INTRODUCTION

IT IS 170 YEARS THIS SUMMER SINCE THE PADDLE STEAMER BRITANNIA LEFT LIVERPOOL'S COBURG DOCK BOUND FOR HALIFAX NOVA SCOTIA AND BOSTON.

The vessel's successful crossing of the mighty North Atlantic Ocean, and its safe arrival in Canada, marked the start of one of the most enduring chapters in the city's rich maritime and mercantile history.

On board the wooden ship departing the Mersey on 4th July 1840 was Samuel Cunard, founder of the company that was to go on to become the most famous passenger line in the world.

The history of the company he created is inextricably linked to Liverpool.

The city remains Cunard Line's spiritual home and visits by the huge modern-day successors to the tiny Britannia have become the stuff of legend.

The most famous and successful Cunarder in history – the legendary QE2 – was planned and designed in the Cunard Building at the Pier Head before entering service in 1969.

Liverpool had to wait 21 years before being able to welcome the transatlantic queen to the city of its conception.

It was worth the wait. More than 1 million people turned out on the banks of the Mersey throughout the day and evening of Tuesday, 24th July 1990 during QE2's maiden call at Liverpool.

The latest Cunarder to call at the port will mark that very special anniversary. On 26th July 2010, Queen Victoria will cross the Mersey Bar to open a new chapter in the history of the line – and the city.

It promises to be another memorable day afloat and ashore.

TONY STOREY,
AUTHOR & EDITOR, CUNARD LIVERPOOL

CUNARD
LIVERPOOL

SPIRITUAL HOME OF THE WORLD'S
MOST FAMOUS OCEAN LINERS

is published by:
Trinity Mirror North West & North Wales
PO Box 48
Old Hall Street,
Liverpool L69 3EB

Trinity Mirror Business Development Director:
Mark Dickinson

Trinity Mirror Sport Media Executive Editor:
Ken Rogers

Cunard Liverpool Editor:
Tony Storey

Design / production:
Colin Harrison

Additional design / production:
Rick Cooke, Vicky Andrews, Paul Dove

Written by:
Tony Storey

Trinity Mirror NW²

© Pictures and text, unless otherwise stated:
Trinity Mirror / Liverpool Daily Post & Echo / Cunard Archive.

The publishers are grateful to the following individuals
and organisations for the assistance given in producing this
commemorative publication: Peter Shanks;
Eric Flounders; Michael Gallagher (Cunard Line);
Captain Paul Wright, *Master*, Queen Victoria;
Maureen Ryan, *Madrina*, Queen Victoria;
Robert Lloyd, *Marine Artist* (www.robertlloyd.com)
and Fincantieri Cantieri Navali Italiani S.p.A.

ISBN 9 781906 802158

FOREWORD

ANOTHER YEAR AND ANOTHER CUNARDER ARRIVES ON THE MERSEY!

I will remember for a long time the welcome our flagship Queen Mary 2 received when she made her maiden call to Liverpool last October – becoming the largest passenger ship ever to sail up the river. And I look forward to the arrival of Queen Victoria on 26th July 2010 as I'm sure she, like Queen Mary 2 and QE2 before her, will receive a welcome that will be just as warm and live long in our memories.

Cunard and Liverpool have shared such a long, fascinating and eventful history. The company was founded in 1839 during the reign of Queen Victoria. And it was on a high tide on the evening of 4th July 1840 – 170 years ago this month – that the first Cunarder, Britannia, began her pioneering maiden voyage to Canada and the United States – thus inaugurating the first regular Atlantic service by steamer.

I can think of no better way to celebrate this milestone than have the Cunard Queen, named after Victoria, visit Liverpool in a year when the fleet will comprise the three largest Cunarders ever built – and a year that will see one of the oldest names in shipping have the youngest fleet afloat.

And Cunarders will continue to visit. Next year will see not one but two of our ocean liners alongside the Pier Head. Queen Elizabeth, which will enter service in just a few months, will make her maiden call on Thursday 8th September while exactly one week later on Thursday 15th September our flagship Queen Mary 2 will make her second call.

But it is worth mentioning that ships from our sister companies, Princess Cruises, Holland America Line, Seabourn and Aida have also been seen on the river in recent years and will continue to be seen in future years.

So let us celebrate this 170th anniversary in style!

PETER SHANKS
PRESIDENT AND MANAGING DIRECTOR
CUNARD LINE

CONTENTS

VOYAGE INTO 170 YEARS OF HISTORY

CUNARD

1839
Samuel Cunard establishes the British and North American Royal Mail Steam Packet Company – known as the Cunard Line – principally to carry the Royal Mail to Canada and the USA.

1840
The 1,154-ton paddle steamer **Britannia**, and three near sisterships, **Acadia**, **Caledonia** and **Columbia**, enter service. These vessels make the Atlantic voyage in 14 days at 8.5 knots and maintain weekly departures from Liverpool.

1852
Cunard's first iron-hulled, screw-driven vessel, the **Andes**, introduced, but not used in the transatlantic service.

1854
Eleven Cunard ships requisitioned for the Crimean War.

1856
The famous Persia built, the company's first iron-hulled transatlantic vessel.

WHEN THE LINER QUEEN VICTORIA CROSSES THE MERSEY BAR FOR THE FIRST TIME ON THE MORNING OF JULY 26TH 2010, SHE WILL MARK AN ASTONISHING MILESTONE IN THE HISTORY OF BOTH CUNARD LINE AND THE CITY OF LIVERPOOL.

The newest Cunarder in the fleet will reach Liverpool almost exactly 170 years after the first ship to bear the great founder's name left the port bound for Halifax, Nova Scotia.

Samuel Cunard himself was on board the paddle steamer Britannia as she pulled away from Coburg Dock to start his line's maiden crossing of the North Atlantic.

The vessel, small enough to fit inside a restaurant on board Cunard Line's current flagship Queen Mary 2, made the crossing in a fortnight. The voyage marked a revolution in the means of communication of the day. This was, after all, a time when mail and newspapers could take weeks to reach parts of the world.

Having proved the relative speed and efficiency of his North Atlantic service, Cunard secured a valuable contract with the Admiralty to run mail on weekly service sailing every Saturday from Liverpool to either Halifax or Boston.

By this time the pioneering engineering in Britannia had been carried across to a fleet of sister ships. Between them these vessels set the course on which Cunard Line has criss-crossed the oceans of the world ever since.

Cunard's first ships were far removed from the luxury associated with them now; indeed, Cunard and luxury were total strangers. Like the man, the ships were plain and practical.

Cabins were small, each divided from the next by a mere partition.

Passengers were responsible for washing their own plate and cutlery, though eating was often far from their minds in inclement weather as they paddled about below decks ankle deep in water. "There's water pouring down the stairs" exclaimed one early passenger to an officer. "We only worry, madam", he replied, "when it's coming up the stairs".

Fresh meat ran out early in each voyage, after which salted was all that was available, and milk was supplied by a hapless cow slung on the deck in a hammock.

Samuel Cunard

*The paddle steamer
Britainnia*

But uncomfortable and basic though they were, Cunard's steamships had two great advantages over sailing ships: firstly, they got the agony over more quickly – 10 days as opposed to six weeks – and secondly, they were steadfastly safe and reliable.

Samuel Cunard himself made safety his priority – and to this day Cunard has never been responsible for the loss of a single passenger or a single mailbag on the Atlantic run.

Cunard's original instruction to his first master, Captain Woodroffe, was simply "Speed is nothing…safety is all that is required" and that has been followed religiously by the company ever since.

Cunard's safety record – which was such that passengers would refuse to board other Line's ships but insist on waiting for the next Cunarder, together with the mail contract, made Cunard profits.

But the company's first excursion into war produced a serious risk to that prosperity. In 1854, 14 Cunard ships – almost the entire fleet – were requisitioned for the Crimean War.

CUNARD

1859
Samuel Cunard created a Baronet in recognition of the Company's service in the Crimean War.

1862
The China the company's first propeller-driven ship. Admiralty permission required to use the ship to carry the Royal Mail as the mail contract stipulates 'paddle steamers'.

202

British and North American Royal Mail Steam Ships,

Appointed by the Admiralty to sail between New York and Liverpool direct—and between Boston and Liverpool, the Boston ships only calling at Halifax to land and receive passengers and Her Majesty's Mails.

The Ships Composing this Line are the following:

Arabia, Capt. Judkins.	*Africa*, Capt. Harrison.
Asia, " Lott.	*Europa*, " Shannon.
Niagara, " Leitch.	*America*, " Lang.
Persia, " Ryrie.	*Cambria*, " Douglas.
Canada, " Stone.	

Proposed Dates of Sailing.

Between Boston and Liverpool.		Between New York and Liverpool.	
FROM LIVERPOOL.	FROM BOSTON.	FROM LIVERPOOL.	FROM NEW YORK.
September 2d,	September 13th,	September 9th,	September 20th,
September 16th,	September 27th,	September 23d,	October 4th,
September 30th,	October 11th,	October 7th,	October 18th,
October 14th,	October 25th,	October 21st,	November 1st,
October 28th,	November 8th,	November 4th,	November 15th'
November 11th,	November 22d,	November 18th,	November 29th,
November 25th,	December 6th,	December 2d,	December 13th,
December 9th,	December 20th,	December 16th,	December 27th,
December 23d,	1855	December 30th,	1855
1855	January 3d,	1855	January 10th,
January 6th,	January 17th,	January 13th,	January 24th,
January 20th,	January 31st,	January 27th,	February, 7th,
February 3d,	February 14th,	February 10th,	February, 21st,
February 17th,	February 28th,	February 24th,	March 7th,
March 3d,	March 14th,	March 10th,	March 21st,
March 17th,	March 28th,	March 24th,	April 4th,
March 31st,	April 11th,	April 7th,	April 18th,
April 14th,	April 25th,	April 21st,	May 2d,
April 28th,	May 9th,	May 5th,	May 16th,
May 12th,	May 23d,	May 19th,	May 30th,
May 26th,	June 6th,	June 2d,	June 13th,
June 9th,	June 20th,	June 16th,	June 27th,
June 23d,	July 4th,,	June 30th,	July 11th,
July 7th,	July 18th,,	July 14th,	July 25th,
July 21st,	August 1st,	July 28th,	August 8th,
August 4th,	August 15th,	August 11th,	August 22d,
August 18th,	August 29th,	August 25th,	September 5th,
September 1st,		September 8th,	

Price of Passage, 1st Cabin, Boston to Liverpool, $110.
" " " 2d " " " " $ 60.
" " " 1st " " " Halifax, $ 20.
" " " 2d " " " " $ 15.
" " " 1st " New York to Liverpool, $130.
" " " 2d " " " " $ 75.

Apply in Boston to S. S. Lewis ; in New York to E. Cunard ; in Halifax to S. Cunard ; in Havre and Paris to Donald Currie ; in Liverpool to D. & C. Mac Iver ; in London to J. B. Ford ; in Glasgow to G. & J. Burns.

from Illustrated American Biography- copyrighted by A D Jones · Jany 1 1855
Engraving by J W Orr
Published by J. Milton Emerson & Co. 1·3·5&7 Spruce St. New York

Samuel Cunard

While the company's contribution to the war effort was remarkable – including transporting all the horses that charged with the Light Brigade – all Cunard mail services on the Atlantic stopped and competition, notably the much-subsidised American Collins Line, won Cunard's lucrative business by default. Crimea gave Samuel Cunard a baronetcy – but it gave Collins a virtual monopoly on the Atlantic.

However, over-expansion and a cavalier attitude to safety did for Collins, which, despite being subsidised by the American government at twice the value of Cunard's mail contract provided 'its ships could outstrip Cunard', went bankrupt in 1858. Cunard regained its pre-eminence.

Samuel Cunard's innate conservatism, which made the founding of the company so remarkable, flared up again in the late 1850s when he steadfastly refused to contemplate the change from paddle wheels to propellers – despite mounting evidence that screw propulsion was more efficient, more powerful and released more space.

He only relented in 1862 with the construction of the China – after first having to seek the permission of the Admiralty as the mail contract specified paddle steamers.

But the China also hinted at a coming decline in the importance of the mail contract, as it was the first ship specifically to cater for emigrants. And so emigration became Cunard's next guarantee of prosperity. Between 1860 and 1900 14 million people emigrated from Europe to the United States; of those, 9 million passed through Liverpool with a sizeable proportion of the immense total making the voyage to America with Cunard.

Cunard's next challenge was the introduction of floating hotel, spearheaded by the newly-formed White Star's Oceanic in 1870.

Where Oceanic had bathtubs, Cunard offered a basin; where Oceanic had central heating, Cunard offered stoves; where Oceanic had taps, Cunard offered jugs; where Oceanic had lamps, Cunard offered candles; and where Oceanic had lavatories, Cunard managed with chamber pots.

Declining revenues forced Cunard to follow suit, and even to innovate. The Servia of 1881 was the first steel Cunarder, the first to be built with an electricity supply, the first to have ensuite bathrooms and the first budgeted to rely solely on passenger revenue. The reliance on the mail diminished even more.

CUNARD

1865
Sir Samuel Cunard dies on 28 April at the age of 78.

1881
The Servia enters service; Cunard's first steel vessel, the first ship in the world to be lighted with electricity, and the first vessel Cunard intended to rely solely on passenger revenue.

1906/07
The liners **Lusitania** and **Mauretania** launched. The latter holds the Blue Riband for the fastest Atlantic crossing for 22 years.

1912
On 15 April the **Carpathia** rescues all the survivors from White Star's Titanic.

1913
The **Aquitania** launched; the first Cunarder with an indoor swimming pool.

Carpathia

CUNARD

1914
The First World War interrupts Cunard's fleet development as Cunard called into active service. Cunard carries over 1 million troops and 10 million tons of cargo for the war cause. Twenty-two ships – including the Lusitania – lost.

1917
The Cunard Building in Liverpool, the company's Head Office until the 1960s, completed.

It was 1902 that saw the virtually unnoticed launch on the Tyne of a minor Cunarder destined for the Mediterranean trade – and also destined to become one of the most famous ships of all time.

She was the 13,600-ton Carpathia which, in 1912, achieved immortality under the command of Captain Arthur Rostron when she sped through icefields in the night, without the benefit of modern radar and at a speed greater than she was supposedly capable of, to rescue all the survivors of the Titanic.

Captain Rostron, later Commodore of the Cunard fleet, master of the Queen Mary and knighted by the King, remarked later that a hand greater than his own guided the little ship that night.

But that was glory yet to come; at the same time as Carpathia was entering service Cunard was looking none too glorious, battered as the company's ageing transatlantic fleet was by ferocious competition from the Germans and Americans.

However, Cunard's fight back led to the introduction of three of the company's most famous ships – Lusitania, Mauretania and Aquitania. These were the first 'floating palaces' in the Cunard fleet – palaces which moved at unprecendented speed. The Mauretania held the Blue Riband record for Transatlantic crossings for 22 years.

Photograph by Howard Davies. Maritime tales at Merseyside Maritime Museum with Stephen Guy.
An etching of the RMS Lusitania c.1911

Again the company was drawn into conflict when its ships were requisitioned for the First World War.

During the four years of carnage, Cunard ships transported over a million men, served as hospital ships, prisoner-of-war ships, food and munitions carriers and as armed merchant cruisers. It was in the latter role that the Carmania had the distinction of taking the first German casualty of the war when she sank the Cap Trafalgar – ironically disguised as Carmania – off South America in November 1914.

Campania, meanwhile, was equipped with a 240-foot long platform and so became the forerunner of today's aircraft carriers.

All in all, over 22 Cunard ships were lost – including the unrequisitioned Lusitania, torpedoed by U20 off the Old Head of Kinsale in 1915 with the loss of 1,200 civilian lives.

Poster depicting Aquitania (1914-1950) leaving New York

A scene from the movie Lusitania: Murder On The Atlantic

The interwar years, bolstered by the addition to the fleet as part of war reparations of the former German vessel Imperator, renamed Berengaria, were successful and lucrative for Cunard – so much so that the company failed to notice the significance of Charles Lindbergh's transatlantic flight in 1927.

Nonetheless, the first real move from reliance on transatlantic revenues was made when, in 1922, Laconia undertook the first-ever World Cruise.

Cunard did not set out to create in 1928 what King George V called "the stateliest ship now in being", and nor did it intend to give birth to a ship which her last Master, Captain John Treasure Jones, said was "the nearest ship ever to be a living being".

It was purely by circumstance that the company produced a ship which more graphically shared the country's triumphs and tribulations, and which was more loved by people who had never even seen her, let alone set foot on her, than any which had gone before.

CUNARD

1919
Cunard awarded the German liner **Imperator** by the British Government, to compensate for the loss of Lusitania. The vessel renamed Berengaria.

1920s /1930s
The heyday of transatlantic shipping, when Cunard's slogan "Getting there is half the fun!" becomes a household phrase.

1922
The **Laconia** undertook the first-ever world cruise.

1934
The 80,744-ton **Queen Mary** launched and after entering service in 1936 soon gains the Blue Riband. The **Queen Mary** is the first merchant vessel to be launched by a member of the Royal family (Her Majesty Queen Mary).

1938
The **Queen Elizabeth** – the largest liner ever built – launched by Her Majesty Queen Elizabeth, later the Queen Mother.

CUNARD

1939

Mauretania (II) enters service. Cunard ships requisitioned once more for war. The Queen Mary and Queen Elizabeth carry between them over 1.5 million troops; Churchill remarks that the two ships helped shorten the war in Europe by at least a year.

LATE 1940S

The Queens begin their transatlantic shuttle, carrying tens of thousands of passengers, from film stars and diplomats to businessmen and tourists.

1949

Cunard's first cruise ship, the Caronia, enters service. She is known as the 'Green Goddess' because of the colour of her hull.

1950S

There are 12 liners in service, carrying one third of all passengers crossing the Atlantic.

1959

The first jet crosses the Atlantic. Air crossings continue to gain passengers at the expense of the great liners. It is in this year when, for the first time, more people cross the Atlantic by air than by sea.

Mauretania

Cunard's intention in 1928 had been simply to replace its ageing transatlantic fleet with a new pair of steamships which could provide a weekly service in each direction – and so meet the growing challenge of German competition on the North Atlantic.

When the first of the pair, Number 534 later to be named Queen Mary, was revealed to be the largest and most powerful ship ever built, the Chairman of Cunard, Sir Percy Bates, diffidently said she was just "the smallest and slowest ship which could accomplish such a service".

Work on Number 534 began at the Clydebank yard of John Brown and Co late in 1930. She was being built at an estimated cost of £6.5 million out of Cunard revenue, without the benefit of any state subsidy.

Almost alone at the time, Cunard operated on the North Atlantic as a commercial concern; every other major line was subsidised to a significant degree by its national government, but Cunard was expected not only to compete but to ensure Britain remained dominant on the North Atlantic without a penny of state aid.

The company did so until the Depression cut revenues of £9 million in 1928 to under £4 million in 1931, and despite Cunard staff on shore and at sea taking a pay cut, work on the construction of Queen Mary stopped just before Christmas 1931.

Immediately 3,640 men in Clydebank – a town where half the wages came from Queen Mary – were thrown out of work. But the ripples were felt by 10,000 ancillary workers further away. They were felt in Stoke-on-Trent, busy working on 200,000 pieces of crockery; in Sheffield, where 100,000 items of cutlery were being crafted; in Walsall, which was producing 400 tons of tubes; in Rugby, manufacturing seven turbo-generators; in Liverpool, producing 2,500 square feet of toughened glass; in Millwall, casting four 20-foot propellers; in Darlington, forging the 190-ton stern frame; in Belfast, working on the 5.5 ton gear wheels; in Halifax, weaving 10 miles of blankets; in St Albans, producing 600 clocks; and in other towns up and down the land making curtains, carpets, anchor chains and furniture. All of them stopped.

The rusting skeleton of Queen Mary, with 80 per cent of the hull rivets in place and £1.5 million already spent, was symbolic of the financial catastrophe which hit both Britain and America.

It was such a graphic symbol of which the general population was so conscious, that members of the public sent thousands of unsolicited donations of money to Cunard in an effort to get the work restarted.

The Government was implored to lend Cunard the capital to complete the ship and get so many back to work – but the Government unswervingly refused – until 1934 that is when, in a complex deal which required Cunard to take over the running of White Star's ailing transatlantic fleet, Neville Chamberlain, then the Chancellor of the Exchequer, agreed to lend Cunard sufficient funds to complete Queen Mary and build her sister, Queen Elizabeth.

Queen Mary in Sydney Harbour Australia

CUNARD

1967
The Queen Elizabeth 2 launched by Her Majesty the Queen.

1969
Maiden voyage of Queen Elizabeth 2, now the only ship offering a scheduled transatlantic service.

1971
Cunard Steamship Company taken over by Trafalgar House PLC after an independent existence of 131 years.

1975
First world cruise of QE2.

1976
Cunard Countess launched.

1977
Cunard Princess launched.

1982
Queen Elizabeth 2 requisitioned by the British Government for the Falkland Islands campaign. Her Majesty Queen Elizabeth the Queen Mother welcomes the ship home. **Cunard Countess** also chartered for use in the conflict.

1983
Cunard purchases top-rated **Sagafjord** and **Vistafjord**, from Norwegian America Cruises, to bring the fleet to five vessels.

CUNARD

1983

Cunard charters Concorde for the first time, thus making use of the company's greatest competitor on the Atlantic, the jet aircraft. Cunard becomes the biggest charterer of Concorde in the world.

1986

Cunard acquires luxury Sea Goddess I and Sea Goddess II vessels, bringing the fleet back to seven ships – the largest number for 25 years.

A six-month £110 million re-engining and refurbishment programme on the QE2, the largest such refit in the history of the merchant marine, undertaken and successfully completed in 1987. HRH the Princess of Wales boards on the ship's return to Southampton.

In May, Her Majesty Queen Elizabeth the Queen Mother boards QE2 to commemorate the 50th anniversary of the Queen Mary's maiden voyage.

And so, on 3rd April 1934, the John Brown workforce, led by a Pipe Band, returned to work and began by removing 130 tons of rust and dozens of nesting crows.

Just five months later Queen Mary, wife of King George V, became the first monarch to launch a merchant ship, a job which she accomplished with a bottle of Australian wine rather than the traditional French champagne.

As she said the words, broadcast over the radio, "I name this ship Queen Mary; may God bless her and all who sail in her", millions of the King's subjects heard his wife's voice for the very first time.

Two hundred thousand spectators watched the launch – and many, on the opposite bank of the Clyde, got wet as an eight foot wave surged across the river when the enormous hull entered the water.

A popular story has it that Cunard's Board had not intended to name the ship Queen Mary, and, to stick to the traditional 'ia' endings prevalent among the Cunard transatlantic fleet, they despatched one of their members, Lord Royden, to ask his friend the King for permission to name the ship 'Queen Victoria'.

Allegedly, he didn't ask directly but intimated that Cunard would like to name the ship after "England's most illustrious Queen". "My wife will be delighted", replied King George, "I will go and tell her now".

A good story – but not true. Cunard had already decided that since the White Star and Cunard transatlantic fleets had been combined under the new banner Cunard White Star, neither the traditional White Star 'ic' ending nor the Cunard 'ia' ending was appropriate. The first ship of the new company needed to break with tradition – and Queen Mary it was intended to be.

The maiden voyage began in Southampton on 27th May 1936, and Queen Mary left to the sounds of bands and ecstatic crowds. On board were the famous bandleader, Henry Hall, scheduled to give a series of live radio broadcasts during the crossing; the virtuoso harmonica player, Larry Adler; and a well-known singer of the time, Frances Day, who performed a song written specially for Queen Mary by Henry Hall, 'Somewhere at Sea'. And, much as she may have liked being at sea, Miss Day did not trust the ship's eggs to be fresh by the end of the voyage so she took along her own hens.

The rapturous welcome in New York on 1st June 1936 marked the completion of the first voyage of four years of glamorous transatlantic service, during which Queen Mary gained the Blue Riband twice for the fastest Atlantic crossing.

Queen Mary leaving New York

The sister ship to Queen Mary, Queen Elizabeth, had a less glorious start. She was launched in 1938 by Queen Elizabeth, wife of George VI – who could not be present himself because the growing pressures of impending war kept him in London – accompanied by Princess Elizabeth, the present Queen, and Princess Margaret.

As fitting-out work was progressing it was decided that not only was Queen Elizabeth a target for German air attacks, but she was also occupying Clydeside shipyard space required for the war effort. She had to move.

The Captain put to sea, with workmen still on board, and once out of the Clyde opened his sealed orders which he expected to instruct him to go to Southampton; instead, he was told to head at full speed to New York. The secret dash was done with the launching gear still affixed to the underside of the ship, and without proper fitments inside.

CUNARD

1988
Her Majesty Queen Elizabeth the Queen Mother boards QE2 for the third time – celebrating the launch of the Queen Elizabeth 50 years earlier.

CUNARD

1990

Cunard celebrates its 150th anniversary. QE2 sent on special Round Britain cruise including her first call at Liverpool and her first return to the Clyde since her launch. It culminates in a rare Spithead Review with Her Majesty the Queen, accompanied by Prince Philip, going on board.

Men who expected to be going home by trains from Southampton within days did not get home for years.

After trooping from Australia, Queen Mary and Queen Elizabeth began bringing American GIs across to Europe in 1942 at full speed and unescorted. Not only were they faster than the U-Boats whose crews had been offered £100,000 by Hitler to sink either of them, but they were faster even than the torpedoes. In summer, 15,000 soldiers were carried on each voyage – such a huge number that the men had to sleep in shifts, observing a strict one-way system on board.

Queen Mary's master, Commodore Sir James Bisset, noted that the ship was so difficult to handle under such circumstances that he was concerned for her stability. All told she made 28 such trips, taking soldiers eastbound and prisoners-of-war westbound, with Queen Elizabeth undertaking a similar number. On three occasions Queen Mary was the nerve-centre of the Empire as Sir Winston Churchill crossed the Atlantic to see President Roosevelt.

The trooping record of the two Queens, together with Aquitania, reduced the duration of the war – according to Churchill – by at least a year.

After the war Queen Mary and Queen Elizabeth had a golden period, doing what they were built to do. This was the era of film stars and royalty being photographed by hundreds of press photographers as they stepped ashore in Southampton or New York. But in the late 1950s the ghost of that Lindbergh flight caught up with Cunard as for the first time, more people crossed the Atlantic by air than by sea. The end was in sight.

Finally, the Queen Mary left New York for the last time on 22nd September 1967 – her 1,001st voyage. This was just two days after the launch by Her Majesty The Queen of Queen Elizabeth 2. During the crossing she passed Queen Elizabeth for the last time, just a mile distant, at a combined speed of 60 knots.

Embarking Australian troops on to Queen Mary during World War 2

CUNARD

1991
Cunard Princess chartered to the US Government for use in the Gulf Conflict as a 'rest and recuperation centre.'

1992
Margaret Thatcher boards QE2 to commemorate the 10th anniversary of the Falklands War.

HRH The Duke of Edinburgh and HRH Prince Edward attend an overnight 'Royal Ball' on QE2 to raise money for the Duke of Edinburgh's Award Scheme.

1993
Cunard enters into a joint venture agreement with Crown Cruise Line involving Crown Dynasty, Crown Jewel and Crown Monarch.

QE2 becomes the first ever ship to be awarded Five Stars by the RAC.

To celebrate the 40th anniversary of the Queen's Coronation, HRH Prince Edward lunches on board QE2 as she sails out of Southampton.

1994
QE2 celebrates her 25th year of service.

QE2 and Vistafjord takes part in the 'D' Day Flotilla.
Crown Monarch leaves the Cunard Fleet.

CUNARD

1994
Cunard purchases the world's highest rated cruise ship, the Royal Viking Sun, for $170 million.

Vistafjord undergoes a £10 million refit and refurbishment.

QE2 completes her £30 million refit which saw changes to the interior – launching the ship into the next century.

1995
Cunard Princess and Crown Jewel leave the Cunard fleet.

Crown Dynasty taken by Cunard on a long-term charter.

Royal Viking Sun Sea Goddess I, Sea Goddess II and Cunard Countess undergo a comprehensive programme of refitting and refurbishment.

QE2 completes one thousand voyages.

1996
During her World Cruise QE2 achieves her four millionth mile – the equivalent of sailing 185 times around the globe.

The Norwegian conglomerate Kvaerner acquires Trafalgar House for £904 million and assumes control of Cunard – this is the second major ownership change for Cunard in its 156 year history.

Having carried 2,114,000 passengers, plus 810,730 military personnel, 19,000 GI brides and 4,000 child evacuees and having travelled 3,794,017 nautical miles, Queen Mary left on her last journey from Southampton on 31st October 1967, bound for her present home in Long Beach California. On board were two double-decker London buses, and the passengers on board delighted in rounding Cape Horn on a bus.

She arrived to an ecstatic welcome in Long Beach where she remains today – officially now a building, rather than one of the greatest ships ever built.

Queen Elizabeth ended her career just a year later in an ignominious fashion, just as she had started it in less triumphant circumstances than Queen Mary. Sold by Cunard in 1968, she eventually ended up in Hong Kong to undergo conversion into a floating university. There, in 1972, a number of mysterious fires broke out simultaneously and, inundated by millions of gallons of water from fire hoses, the ship turned over and sank – her side visible above the water.

The sale of Queen Mary and Queen Elizabeth was the nadir in Cunard's fortunes. Towards the end the ships had been criss-crossing the Atlantic virtually empty – on one voyage Queen Elizabeth had only 200 passengers – and in so doing they were losing the company £4 million a year each.

And yet, in the face of all evidence to the contrary and in what seemed to many an act of lunacy equal only to Samuel Cunard's original madness in establishing the company, the Cunard board – as it pensioned off two transatlantic liners which had been defeated by the jet aircraft – was planning to construct another transatlantic liner.

Right: The bridge is lowered into place on QE2

Queen Elizabeth on an early voyage

And so Queen Elizabeth 2, a true transatlantic liner with a service speed of 28.5 knots and a 1.5 inch thick hull but which, with its ability to navigate both Panama and Suez could be a cruise ship too, was launched by the Queen in 1967.

She was already famous when she slid down the slipway as a result of intense press speculation about her name, secret to the last (Sir Winston Churchill and Princess Anne had been among the bookies' favourites). And from that point she has never been out of public scrutiny, remaining the most famous ship in the world.

QE2 – as she rapidly became – did not have an auspicious start. Her Keel Laying in 1965 was delayed by three days as the crane destined to place the keel in place toppled over instead. On her sea trials in 1968 recurring turbine problems were followed by a total breakdown off the Canaries, as a result of which QE2 limped into her homeport on her first call at Southampton in January 1969. Cunard refused to accept delivery, six advertised cruises were cancelled – and the

1996
Royal Viking Sun is 'relaunched' in Dover after significant repairs following her grounding.

Sagafjord withdrawn from Cunard service and chartered to Transocean Cruises of Germany; subsequently sold to

CUNARD

1996

Cunard Countess sold to Awani Cruises of Indonesia.

QE2 completes a £12 million refit in Southampton, the first time a UK yard had been used for 13 years.

Cunard become the first cruise line to reveal their Millennium itineraries.

1997

QE2 commences six (instead of five) day Atlantic crossings allowing the ship to take the more leisurely route between Europe and America.

The management / charter contract of Cunard Dynasty is ended and the vessel transfers to Norwegian Cruise Line. This completes Cunard's strategy of offering minimum five-star ships and positions the company as the top cruise line in the world.

A fund-raising event for the Red Cross, which was to have been attended by the late Diana, Princess of Wales, held on board QE2 in Southampton. Guests include Cherie Blair, Elizabeth Dole and Lord Attenborough.

Constant refits and refurbishments maintained QE2's luxurious lifestyle

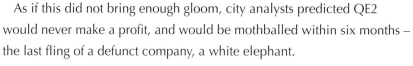

As if this did not bring enough gloom, city analysts predicted QE2 would never make a profit, and would be mothballed within six months – the last fling of a defunct company, a white elephant.

How wrong the analysts were!

The most famous ship in the world sailed serenely on for 41 years, calling at Liverpool nine times to maintain the tradition started in 1840.

And what a dramatic 41 years they were.

In 1972, a threat was made by an American extortionist to blow up QE2 in mid-Atlantic by means of suicide accomplices on board, unless a ransom was paid.

Although the ship already had comprehensive search routines in place, as a precaution Cunard arranged with the Ministry of Defence for SAS personnel to be parachuted into the sea near to QE2. A further search was carried out, but no explosives were found. However, the extortionist was caught and ended up in prison on a 20-year sentence.

A Sea King helicopter lands on board QE2 during the Falklands campaign

Just a year later, according to the former President of Egypt, Anwar Sadat, Colonel Gadaffi planned to torpedo QE2 as she passed through the Mediterranean – and only Sadat's last-minute intervention prevented the attack. In 1976 three members of the IRA were arrested trying to take explosives onboard QE2.

On 4th May 1982, en route to Southampton from Philadelphia, Queen Elizabeth 2 was requisitioned by the Government for service in the Falklands Campaign and so joined the ranks of the great Cunarders called upon to serve their country.

Conversion work to prepare the ship for trooping duties began the following day.

Helicopter landing pads were constructed on the Quarter Deck forward from the Bridge and aft over the two swimming pools – the former possibly constituting, when the ship was travelling at speed, one of the most hazardous landing areas any pilot could wish to encounter.

CUNARD

1997
Vistafjord and Sea Goddess I complete refurbishment programme.

Cunard relocates its global headquarters to Miami after being based in New York for 30 years.

Cunard's five-ship fleet receives the highest ratings by Berlitz 'Complete Guide to Cruising and Cruise Ships'. Four ships are ranked number one in their respective categories.

QE2 celebrates the 30th anniversary of her launch by HM The Queen on 20 September 1967.

1998
Nelson Mandela sails on QE2 from Durban to Cape Town – the first time a Head of State has travelled on board since HM The Queen in 1990.

May, a Carnival Corporation-led consortium, purchases Cunard from Kvaerner for $500 million and merges the company with Seabourn Cruise Line to form Cunard Line Limited.

In June the new company announces 'Project Queen Mary' – a proposal to build the biggest passenger liner ever.

HISTORY OF THE CUNARD LINE

CUNARD

1998

In September Royal Viking Sun completes her refurbishment programme, followed by Sea Goddess II in October.

Also in October the company announces the reorganisation of the two fleets and the renaming of Vistafjord. The reorganisation, effective from December 1999, includes:

The renaming of Royal Viking Sun, Sea Goddess I and Sea Goddess II as Seabourn Sun, Seabourn Goddess I and Seabourn Goddess II and their transfer to the Seabourn fleet.

The renaming of Vistafjord as Caronia. Together with QE2, Caronia forms the basis of the 'new' Cunard Line fleet.

Cunard Line Limited sweeps the board in the 1999 Berlitz 'Complete Guide to Cruising and Cruise Ships' with the top seven places being taken by either a Cunard or Seabourn ship. QE2 Grill accommodation receives the highest ratings.

Flagship of the British Merchant Fleet in the South Atlantic war zone

Valuable paintings and furniture were removed, piping for refuelling at sea laid through passenger areas, and hardboard placed over carpets.

Equipment, rations, vehicles, fuel and spare parts were loaded aboard – so much that a great deal had to be stored on the open deck.

To man the ship, Cunard asked for volunteers from among its employees to go to the war zone; it required 650, and it got over 1,000.

On 12th May, 3,000 men of the Fifth Infantry Brigade comprising units of the Scots Guards, the Welsh Guards and the Gurkha Rifles, along with naval personnel, came aboard and QE2, under the command of Captain Peter Jackson, put to sea and headed south.

On the journey southwards from Freetown, the only port of call, every one of the liner's portholes was covered with black plastic to provide a total blackout: from being the ocean's brightest star, QE2 – for her own safety – became the darkest.

CUNARD

1999

On 14 April a lunch is held on board QE2 in Southampton to commemorate the 30th anniversary of the ship's maiden transatlantic crossing (2-7 May 1969).

Carnival Corporation acquires the 32% of Cunard it did not already own, thus taking control of 100% of the company.

Cunard Line Limited once again triumphs in the 2000 Berlitz 'Complete Guide to Cruising and Cruise Ships' with the top six places being taken by either a Cunard or Seabourn ship.

The fleet re-organistion takes place with major refurbishments being completed on QE2, Caronia and Seabourn Sun.

2000

By the end of 2000, the $27 million programme of refurbishment of Seabourn Pride, Seabourn Spirit and Seabourn Legend is complete. All three ships received unique 'French Balconies'.

2001

In February Pamela Conover becomes the first woman at the helm of Cunard when she is appointed President and Chief Operating Officer.

On 22nd May news came through of the loss of the Atlantic Conveyor, a Cunard ship also serving in the Falklands Campaign. This was a particularly bleak day as many of the QE2's crew had friends aboard the Atlantic Conveyor; the news of heavy loss of life caused enormous sadness.

On the last leg of the outbound voyage, on 23rd May, the navigation lights were extinguished and the radar turned off in order to silence the ship electronically.

This deprived QE2's navigating officers of a vital aid, and put them back almost half a century. But the situation became particularly grave once the ship entered icefields north of South Georgia. Huge icebergs were encountered on the night of 26th May – many bigger than the ship – and to compound a serious situation, fog reduced visibility to less than a mile.

CUNARD

2001

On 26 March, Seabourn announces the transfer of Seabourn Sun to Holland America Line in April 2002. Seabourn Sun to be renamed Prinsendam.

Separate management structures established for Cunard Line and Seabourn Cruise Line in the Miami Head Office.

On 13 July, Seabourn announces the sale of both Seabourn Goddess I and Seabourn Goddess II to a group of Norwegian investors.

In October Cunard announces the redeployment of Caronia to the British cruise market effective in May 2002. The on board product to become British and the currency to be sterling.

QE2 undergoes further refurbishment in November/December.

On 17 December Cunard announces the construction of a 90,000-ton vessel. 'The New Cunarder' will enter service in January 2005 and be dedicated to the British cruise market.

2002

On 16 January the first steel is cut to mark the formal start of construction of Queen Mary 2.

On 27th May, QE2 anchored in Cumberland Bay, South Georgia, where the tricky job of transferring troops and supplies to other vessels began. In total darkness, requisitioned trawlers carried out the enormously difficult task of shuttling between the blacked-out vessels.

The transfer of troops and stores was completed on 29th May, after which 640 survivors of HMS Ardent, Coventry and Antelope came aboard for the journey back to Ascension Island.

Shortly before the scheduled day of arrival at Ascension on 4th June, orders were received from the Ministry of Defence that QE2 was to proceed instead to Southampton with the survivors.

At 0900 hours on 11th June, QE2 passed the Needles. Two hours later the survivors of Ardent, Coventry and Antelope mustered on deck to be greeted by Her Majesty Queen Elizabeth the Queen Mother, waving from the Britannia. As a further gesture, the Queen Mother radioed a message of welcome to QE2.

So finally, 12½ days after leaving South Georgia and almost 15,000 miles since first setting out from Southampton over a month earlier, Queen Elizabeth 2 was home, having done what was required of her in the service of the country.

QE2 arrives home after South Atlantic service

2002

On 13 May Cunard confirms that QE2 will be removed from transatlantic service in April 2004 and will be deployed on cruise service out of Southampton. QM2 will assume the role of Cunard's transatlantic carrier at this time.

Lady Thatcher lunches on board QE2 on 14 June to commemorate the 20th anniversary of the Falklands War.

On 4 July the keel is laid for **Queen Mary 2.**

2003

On 21 March Queen Mary 2 is floated out of the building dock.

On 31 March Cunard announces that 'The New Cunarder' will be named **Queen Victoria.**

On 12 July the keel is laid for **Queen Victoria.**

In December, Queen Mary 2 is handed over to Cunard and arrives in Southampton.

2004

On 8 January Queen Mary 2 is named by Her Majesty the Queen.

On 12 January RMS Queen Mary 2 sails on her Maiden Voyage.

RMS Queen Mary 2 departs Southampton on 16 April on her first transatlantic crossing to New York.

But not all the highlights of QE2's career have been so dramatic.

In 1990, during her first call at Liverpool, over one million people turned out to welcome her. Later in the same week, the Queen boarded in Southampton – her first visit since the ship's introduction to service.

In 1983, conscious of QE2's pulling power, Cunard decided to invest £110 million in replacing the 20-year old steam turbine engines with diesel electric engines.

On 20th October 1986, QE2 left New York for her last ever crossing as a steamship: QE2's last and Cunard's last. Cunard had been the first company to offer a timetabled steamship service across the Atlantic, and, despite war, depression and foreign competition, it was now the last to do so. But QE2 re-emerged the following year to carry on that tradition – with a new propulsion system and a renewed life expectancy.

It was generally thought at that point that QE2 would be the last ever transatlantic liner. When she's gone, everybody said, there will never be another. And yet.

One of the first things announced by Carnival Corporation when they purchased Cunard in 1998 was the construction of a new transatlantic liner to follow in the glorious wake of Britannia, Mauretania, Aquitania, Queen Mary, Queen Elizabeth and QE2. A heritage everyone thought was bound to die lives on – together with Cunard Line's unique connection to Liverpool.

2004

On 25 April both RMS Queen Mary 2 and QE2 meet in New York – the first time that two Cunard Queens have been berthed in the port since March 1940.

On 1 May both Queens arrive in Southampton – the first time two Cunard Queens have been in the company's home port since 1967. QE2 relinquishes the title of flagship to RMS Queen Mary 2. QE2 is the longest serving Cunard flagship.

5 November QE2 becomes Cunard's longest serving express liner having completed 35 years, six months and three days of service – taking the record from Aquitania.

2005

Having completed 36 years, four months and two days record in service QE2 becomes the longest serving Cunard ship ever on 4 September, taking the record from the Scythia which served from 1921 to 1957.

2006

On 19 May the keel is laid for Queen Victoria.

2007

QE2, undertaking her 25th World Cruise, meets Queen Mary 2, undertaking her Maiden World Cruise, in Sydney Harbour.

QE2 passes Crosby beach

CUNARD

2007

Sale of QE2 to the Government of Dubai announced.

QE2 undertakes a 'lap-of-honour' around the UK to mark the 40th anniversary of her 1967 launch. The voyage includes a maiden call to the Tyne, a visit to the Clyde exactly 40 years to the day and a return visit to Liverpool.

On 10 December **Queen Victoria** is named by Her Royal Highness The Duchess of Cornwall and departs on her Maiden Voyage two days later.

2008

QE2 leaves Southampton for the final time on 11 November and sails her Final Voyage to Dubai, where she is handed over to her new owners on 27 November.

2009

The keel for **Queen Elizabeth** is laid on 2 July. **Queen Mary 2** marks 5th anniversary of service with a Round Britain cruise from Edinburgh, Glasgow, Liverpool, Cork and Cherbourg.

2010

Queen Victoria marks 170th anniversary of Britannia's first Atlantic crossing with call at Liverpool.

Queen Elizabeth due to enter service in October.

QUEEN VICTORIA'S VENETIAN HERITAGE

THE CHARMING AND BEAUTIFUL CITY OF VENICE WAS WHERE
QUEEN VICTORIA STARTED HER LIFE IN A SPRAWLING
SHIPYARD A WATER TAXI RIDE AWAY FROM THE GRAND CANAL.

State-of-the-art cruise liners are not built in many more inspiring places
in the world.

The departure of each new ship from Fincantieri's Marghera yard offers
unrivalled photographic opportunities for the teams marketing these
luxury liners.

Incongruous as it may at first appear, these floating places look strangely
well placed as they purr past the tidal edge of St Mark's Square and many
of the city's other famous and most photographed landmarks.

Once Cunard's precise design requirements had been finalised, it took
just two years to build the ship

At 90,000, the ship was of slightly greater tonnage than had been
planned when work originally started on the hull.

The keel of Queen Victoria is placed in position

In order to accommodate more suites and fine dining restaurant capacity (the famous Cunard Grills experience), Cunard's parent company switched the original order to another of its famous brands, P & O Cruises.

Thus, the hull that started life as Cunard's Queen Victoria became P & O Cruises' Arcadia and launched in 2005.

At the time of the re-assigned order for the new Cunard liner, Carnival Corporation & plc Chairman and CEO Micky Arison commented:

"With these extensive modifications, Queen Victoria will incorporate the 'grand ocean liner' style of the Queen Mary 2 and Queen Elizabeth 2, as well as the signature design elements and culinary experiences that have earned Cunard its position as the pre-eminent luxury cruise operator," Arison said. "At the same time, the re-engineered Queen Victoria will serve as Cunard's Super Liner of the future," he added.

The agreement with Fincantieri included a significant redesign of the Queen Victoria, for which the order had previously been announced in April 2004. The vessel was lengthened by 11 metres and its tonnage increased to 90,000 with its passenger capacity increased to 2,000. The redesign brought the all-in price to €340 million plus $95 million (US).

Arison's huge Carnival Corporation had established a strong relationship with the Italian industrialists.

By the time work proper started on the redesigned Queen Victoria, Fincantieri yards had delivered 29 ships to the various Carnival brands.

The shopping spree was driven by phenomenal growth in the worldwide cruise sector and cost a cool $10 billion (US).

With such buying power, the need to redesign, lengthen and strengthen the hull of the new Cunarder was treated as little more than a slight inconvenience by the builders. They may not quite be able to offer Mr Arison a buy one get one free deal, but Carnival's carefully planned procurement strategy inevitably allowed hard deals to be struck.

In common with other yards around the world, Fincantieri's build process is based on the separate construction of hundreds of individual steel blocks and sections which are then assembled in a dry dock.

*Taking shape:
Queen Victoria
during construction*

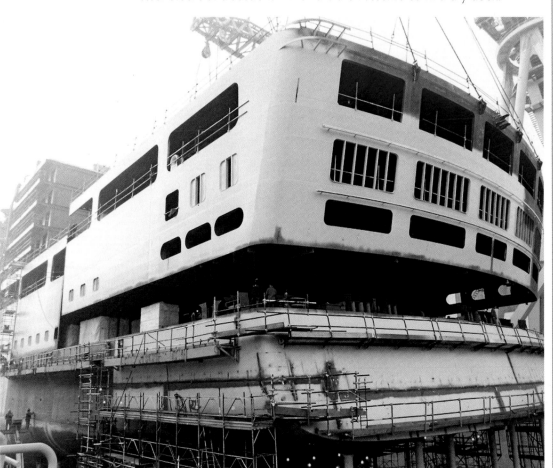

Above: Lifted into place... an entire section of a luxurious lounge is added to Queen Victoria

Rather than a conventional launch down a slip way, each new hull built in this way first meets the water when the dry dock gates are opened and the basin floods.

The start of construction is marked by a keel-laying ceremony.

For Queen Victoria this took place in 2006. The first section was made up of six pre-manufactured blocks with a combined weight of 325 tons.

Speed and efficiency of build is critical to the successful completion of any order, thus this block, and subsequent sections, arrive at the basin ready to be lifted into place with tons of ancillary equipment, piping and ducting already in place.

The ship was assembled in 80 similar sections. Each lift by the yard's distinctive yellow cranes was meticulously planned. The wheelhouse – 34 metres across – was built as a single section and lowered into position 26 metres above sea level.

By September 2006, 10,500 tons of steel had been erected in the dock and 33 sections were already in place. The main engines and the liner's distinctive bulbous bow (designed to cut through the waves) were in place.

Queen Victoria has six diesel engines, four with 16 cylinders each and two with 12 cylinders each. These propel the ship, and provide all onboard power, via a state-of-the-art system which features propellers attached to huge pods hanging off the stern of the ship in a configuration, sometimes likened to that of an outboard motor on a speed boat.

Each pod can be turned through 360 degrees and locked at any position. This, combined with the capacity for the pitch of the propeller blades to be varied, gives the giant liner exceptional manoeuvrability.

Beneath the water line, set low in the bow of the ship, a set of thrusters complete the power package at the Captain's disposal.

In the way new buildings ashore host "topping out" ceremonies, new vessels built for Carnival Corporation feature a special ceremony at the end of the construction phase of the build.

This usually involved a specially selected set of coins being placed at the foot of the ship's mast – often in a display case that is then welded shut.

Senior representatives of the builders and operators are joined at these ceremonies by a VIP guest. At Italian shipyards this person is known as the madrina.

*That's my cabin!
Accommodation
blocks take
their place*

*Above: A forward
section is lowered
into place*

Former Cunard Line President Carol Marlow at the keel laying of Queen Victoria

At the conclusion of the welding ceremony, valves on the dry dock gates are opened and the basin floods in the course of several hours allowing the ship to float for the first time.

Queen Victoria's float out took place on 15th January 2007.

Cunard's then Managing Director, Carol Marlow, was joined by Maureen Ryan as guest of honour at the event.

Maureen joined Cunard in 1963 and is the only known person to have served on all Cunard Queens: Queen Mary, Queen Elizabeth, QE2 and Queen Mary 2.

In recognition of her outstanding service and achievement, Cunard bestowed on Maureen the honour, in Italian tradition, of being madrina to the new ship.

The first ceremony involved the welding of two coins beneath the mast. Two coins chosen were a Euro (symbolising the fact that the ship was being built in Italy) and a gold Queen Victoria sovereign with St George slaying the dragon on the reverse side.

Carol Marlow explained the significance of the second coin to assembled guests on the top deck of the ship.

She said: "Cunard came into being at the very beginning of the Victorian era – Queen Victoria had been on the throne for only three years when Samuel Cunard's first ship set sail. And there followed, throughout her reign, a huge expansion in the Cunard fleet until by the end of it the company was the pre-eminent force in British shipping. Today the company is probably the most famous name in shipping and the birth of this great liner confirms for all to see, the continuing renaissance of the great name of Cunard. The Cunard lion roars again!"

After the coin ceremony, a further ceremony took place on the dockside at which the ship was blessed and a bottle of Italian prosecco smashed against the hull. The valves of the dry dock were then opened.

Corrado Antonini, Chairman of Fincantieri, told guests:

"Our company is the heir to the Italian shipbuilding industry and the world leader in cruise ship construction and believes, as Cunard does, in the possibility and the need of actively matching tradition and innovation. Building a liner for Cunard is a special achievement for Fincantieri and takes us right to our roots, fostering both our determination to build once again a passenger ship of high technological content and unmistakable style, reflecting the best of the industry and tailored to the needs and requirements of the owner".

A true Cunarder...
the distinct brick red
funnel is added to
Queen Victoria

By the time guests assembled on the dockside for their coach journey back to the city's Marco Polo airport and a flight back to the UK, Fincantieri workers were preparing to resume work fitting out the vessel.

The day of pomp and ceremony was over.

Just eight months later, Cunard Line issued a brief statement confirming that the new ship had passed her final sea trials with flying colours.

The statement read:

'Cunard's new liner, Queen Victoria, has successfully completed her sea trials. She is now back in the shipyard for the final phase of her outfitting.'

Carol Marlow, then Cunard's President and Managing Director, commented:

"Queen Victoria has successfully completed her first venture out to sea and now, back at the yard, we will bring her magnificent public spaces and luxurious suites and staterooms to life by adding intriguing artwork, elegant public room features and classical furnishings".

Final fitting out work continued apace in the weeks that followed until, on 24th November 2007, the completed vessel was ready to be handed over to Cunard.

Senior politicians at the time in both Italy and UK attended the ceremony.

Italian Prime Minister, Romano Prodi, and the Under Secretary of State, Department for Transport, Jim Fitzpatrick MP, were present at the high profile Handover Ceremony.

Just after 1100 hours, following speeches, the Italian flag was ceremonially lowered and the Red Ensign raised, marking the point at which another magnificent Cunard liner entered the Register of British Shipping. The event was given a British emphasis by the presence of the Band of the Scots Guards, flown out specially to perform on board throughout the day.

Carol Marlow said: "This ceremony to mark the completion of the ship, and our acceptance of delivery, is just the first of a number of significant events over the next few weeks – including the ship's official naming by HRH The Duchess of Cornwall, in the presence of HRH The Prince of Wales, in Southampton on Monday 10th December. I'm certain the British will take this truly magnificent ship to their hearts, as they have all the Cunard Queens".

Queen Victoria sailed from the shipyard on 30th November under the command of her first Captain Paul Wright and bound for Southampton – and a date with Royalty.

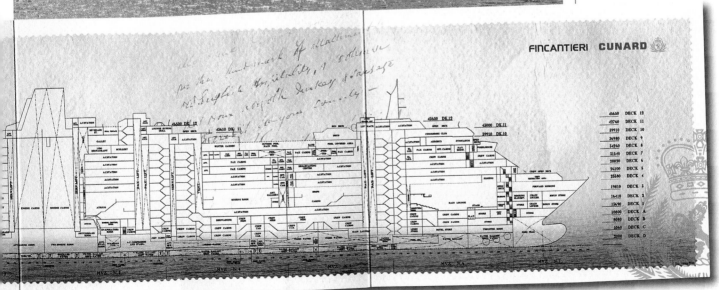

THE WRIGHT MAN FOR CAPTAIN

CAPTAIN PAUL WRIGHT WAS APPOINTED QUEEN VICTORIA'S FIRST MASTER IN OCTOBER 2006.

He is a veteran of Cunard Line having served the company and its vessels for more that 27 years.

Captain Wright is married and lives in Cornwall. He first went to sea in 1965 as a cadet with Shell Tankers, but quickly progressed to passenger ships in 1969 when he joined Canadian Pacific.

His first appointment with Cunard was to Cunard Countess, since when he has served on Cunard Princess, Sagafjord and Cunard Dynasty.

In 1999 Captain Wright was promoted to Captain of Cunard's then flagship Queen Elizabeth 2 where he served until construction of the largest liner ever built, Queen Mary 2. He oversaw construction of the ship in St. Nazaire prior to commission, and in 2004 was appointed Master of Queen Mary 2, alternating with the former Commodore of the Fleet, Ron Warwick.

Asked what his most memorable moments at sea have been, Captain Wright cites two: when he brought QE2 into New York for the first time after the 11 September attack on the World Trade Centre in 2001, and bringing Queen Mary 2 into Hamburg on her maiden call when half a million people turned out to greet the ship.

Captain Wright says:

"Bringing Queen Victoria into Southampton for the first time gave me a third most memorable event. Nothing stirs the imagination quite as much as a new Cunarder arriving in port for the first time. She is a magnificent vessel built in true Cunard style".

OPULENCE AND GLAMOUR AT SEA AND ASHORE

Top: A figure of Victory stands on top of the company's war memorial in front of the building

Middle: An old house sits in front of the Cunard Building, around 1950

Bottom: Intricate detail of carvings adorn the outside of the building

CUNARD LINE'S FORMER WORLD HEADQUARTERS AT THE PIER HEAD REMAIN A SHORESIDE REMINDER OF THE OPULENCE AND GLAMOUR ASSOCIATED WITH LINER TRAVEL AROUND THE GLOBE.

Built during the First World War, the middle of Liverpool's Three Graces – so named after the daughters of Zeus who personified grace, beauty and charm – was the final building of the three to be completed.

Today, although the interior of the building has been sub-let to various companies and organisations, there is no mistaking the purpose for which it was designed and built.

As well as being a ticketing office and embarkation hall for the passenger line, it also housed Cunard's complete shore-based teams of designers, engineers and managers who ran the global operation from the Mersey waterfront.

Today, the building's historic maritime pedigree offers a fascinating insight into how Liverpool was once established as a focal point of world passenger trade.

The ground floor main hall served as the main passenger embarkation facility where guests exited by the imposing entrance straight on to Pier Head and their waiting Liner.

The building was constructed on the site of the former George's Dock and a section of Liverpool's original sea wall has been retained deep in the basement of the building. Elsewhere in the basement huge vaults, each named after a

serving Cunard Liner, were used for the safekeeping of passengers' valuables.

Huge luggage storage areas are also retained with row upon row of wooden shelving still bearing the names of famous Cunard ships. On the top floor of the building a magnificent hall was reserved for the use of First Class passengers who could enjoy afternoon tea dances while waiting for their Liners to be readied.

The building is made of reinforced concrete, clad in Portland stone. The stonework was designed to be enhanced by the inevitable accumulation of soot. Subsequent cleaning has evened out the intended contrast of light and dark.

The frieze is carved with the shields of countries allied in the First World War. A stately marble-lined corridor with Doric columns links the North and South entrances, giving access to lifts and stairs.

The Cunard Building was the centre of Britain's cruise ship industry for many years, a land based reflection of the glory and wealth of cruise liners. Its design was influenced by grand Italian palaces and reflects the Greek neo-classical revival.

In the forecourt of the Cunard Building is the company's war memorial; a slender column on top of which is a bronze figure of VICTORY.

Above the doors leading directly to the waterfront there remains a large lion rampant on a globe – Cunard Line's emblem.

*Cunard Building
overlooks the newly opened
Liverpool Link Canal
Picture Andrew Teebay.*

*Liverpool waterfront minus the Cunard
Building. Picture courtesy
of Shelagh Warren of Hightown.*

A DATE WITH ROYALTY

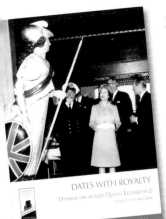

DATES WITH ROYALTY
DINNER ON BOARD QUEEN ELIZABETH 2

DATES WITH ROYALTY HAVE LONG BEEN A PART OF CUNARD LINE HISTORY AND THE SPECTACULAR NAMING CEREMONY FOR QUEEN VICTORIA WAS TO SEE THESE LINKS STRENGTHENED STILL FURTHER.

The ship was due to arrive in its home port of Southampton for the first time on 6th December 2007, marking the start of a hectic period of inaugural celebrations culminating in the official naming ceremony during the afternoon of Monday 10th December.

The following day, surrounded by fireworks, the ship would sail on its maiden voyage.

This 10-night voyage called at ports famed for their Christmas markets: Rotterdam (for Amsterdam), Copenhagen (overnight call), Oslo, Hamburg and Zeebrugge (for Bruges). Fares ranged from £999 to £8,679 per person, and the voyage was fully-booked very shortly after going on sale in 2006.

But before the first fare-paying guests embarked and settled into their staterooms, Cunard's new queen was to be officially named by Her Royal Highness The Duchess of Cornwall in the presence of His Royal Highness The Prince of Wales.

The boom in the popularity of cruising among British holidaymakers in the last decade has driven a huge programme of shipbuilding by the major cruise lines keen to meet the increasing demand.

New ships were being floated out of construction yards on a regular basis with owners and operators seeking to ensure the naming of each new ship secured as much media interest as possible.

For some during the first decade of the 21st century, a form of celebrity endorsement has been chosen as the best way of capturing interest from publishers and broadcasters.

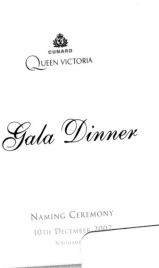

CUNARD
QUEEN VICTORIA

Gala Dinner

NAMING CEREMONY
10TH DECEMBER 2007
SOUTHAMPTON

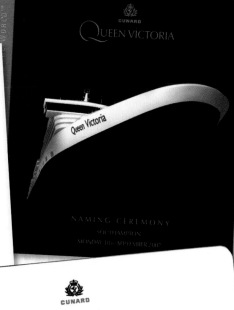

CUNARD
QUEEN VICTORIA

Queen Victoria

NAMING CEREMONY
SOUTHAMPTON
MONDAY 10TH DECEMBER 2007

CUNARD

CAROL MARLOW
PRESIDENT & MANAGING DIRECTOR OF CUNARD LINE
REQUESTS THE PLEASURE OF THE COMPANY OF

AT THE NAMING CEREMONY OF

QUEEN VICTORIA

BY

HER ROYAL HIGHNESS THE DUCHESS OF CORNWALL
IN THE PRESENCE OF
HIS ROYAL HIGHNESS THE PRINCE OF WALES

AT THE CITY CRUISE TERMINAL, SOUTHAMPTON
ON MONDAY 10TH DECEMBER 2007
FOLLOWED BY A GALA OVERNIGHT ON BOARD

R.S.V.P
Queen Victoria Events
PO Box 50463
London, W8 9BZ

Naming Ceremony: 3.30pm
Gala Reception: 6.30pm
Dinner: 8pm

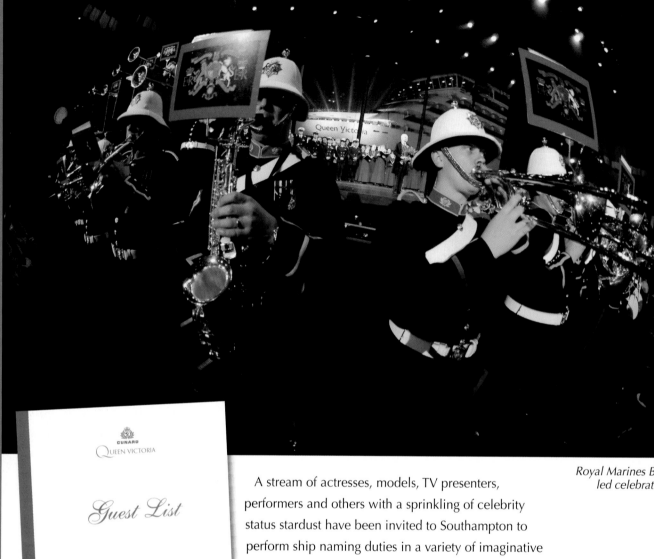

*Royal Marines Band
led celebrations*

CUNARD
QUEEN VICTORIA

Guest List

NAMING CEREMONY
10TH DECEMBER 2007
SOUTHAMPTON

A stream of actresses, models, TV presenters, performers and others with a sprinkling of celebrity status stardust have been invited to Southampton to perform ship naming duties in a variety of imaginative productions.

But none of the events staged by Cunard Line's rival operators bore the splendour and status of a Royal Naming Ceremony – a fact not lost on the US media.

North American journalists descended in strength on Southampton ensuring an important part of Cunard's global market was aware of the arrival of a new Queen in the famous fleet.

Cunard's then President Carol Marlow had announced the latest date with Royalty on 10th September 2007.

A statement issued that day read: "Cunard Line is delighted to announce that Their Royal Highnesses, The Prince of Wales and The Duchess of Cornwall, will attend a ceremony in Southampton on 10th December 2007, to mark the introduction of Cunard's new 90,000-ton liner Queen Victoria. At this ceremony, Her Royal Highness The Duchess of Cornwall will perform the naming of the ship.

HRH The Duchess of Cornwall and HRH The Prince of Wales are welcomed by Carol Marlow

"This naming will be a milestone in both Cunard and British maritime history and will be a major event of worldwide interest, with over 2,000 VIP guests from around the globe in attendance at the prestigious ceremony.

Carol Marlow, President and Managing Director of Cunard Line, comments: "This will be an historic occasion. We are most honoured that Their Royal Highnesses have accepted our invitation and that Her Royal Highness will name our newest Cunarder. Every one of our Cunard Queens has been named by a member of the Royal Family and we are therefore delighted that Queen Victoria will follow in that tradition. In addition, this particular ceremony will mark the beginning of a new era, as it will be the first time in our history that we will have three Cunard Queens in service at the same time.

"Queen Victoria will not only be a classic Cunard ocean liner offering the very best of our heritage and traditions, but will also be the second largest Cunarder the company has ever built. She will be in Southampton for four days, during which time over 7,000 guests from around the world will visit the ship. She will depart on her Maiden Voyage on Tuesday 11th December 2007."

Three Tenors take centre stage

Welcome Ma'am

While the ship herself took centre stage alongside the City Cruise Terminal in Southampton, guests attending the gala event were ushered in a specially-built auditorium on the quayside.

The huge structure accommodated more than 2,000 people and was lavishly decorated and dressed in the style of the ship's own Royal Court Theatre.

The massive temporary theatre also included its very own Royal Box with the best seats in the house reserved for the Naming Party being hosted by, among others, Carnival Corporation and plc Chairman and CEO Micky Arison and Cunard Line's President and Managing Director Carol Marlow.

Stewards and Stewardesses from the ship were assisted in ushering duties by schoolchildren from Southampton City Beaver Colony dressed as Cunard Line Bell Boys.

At precisely 3.30pm the Band of Her Majesty's Royal Marines, Portsmouth and Commando Training Centre Royal Marines under the direction of Lieutenant Colonel C J Davis, Principal Director of Music, Royal Marines, struck up the National Anthem to begin the ceremony.

The National Anthem was followed by a specially-arranged Cunard Fanfare for Trumpeters to mark the arrival of the VIP party in the Royal Box.

Carol Marlow addressed the audience.

"Your Royal Highnesses, my Lords, Mr Mayor, distinguished guests.

"As many of you may know, Cunard Line will now have a three-ship fleet; Queen Elizabeth 2, launched in 1967; Queen Mary 2, named in 2004; and now just three years later a new Queen. And, as we have just announced, another new vessel, Queen Elizabeth will join the fleet in 2010.

"I mention these dates with a purpose. You will not have failed to notice that the world had to wait for 37 years after the launch of QE2 for Cunard to build its next ocean liner. 37 years! Thirty-seven years which many commentators felt demonstrated beyond doubt that Cunard, once the greatest name in shipping, was in terminal decline and being overtaken by new 'modern' shipping companies.

"But look at us now! Three magnificent new ships in the space of just six years!

"This is the revival, the renaissance of that great name; the Cunard lion roars again.

"All of which makes it singularly appropriate that the ship which Her Royal Highness The Duchess of Cornwall has graciously agreed to name today, will be named after the monarch, during whose reign the company saw its first spectacular expansion.

"The Queen to whom I refer, came to the throne in 1837 and Cunard was established just two years later. From a shaky start, with just four tiny paddle steamers, the company went on to become one of the pre-eminent names in world shipping and, by the end of that monarch's long and fruitful reign, was planning the huge four-funnelled floating palaces which we would recognise today as the first truly glamorous, and elegant express transatlantic liners.

Kathrine Jenkins celebrates the naming of Queen Victoria

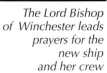

The Lord Bishop of Winchester leads prayers for the new ship and her crew

"It is, therefore, also completely appropriate that this latest addition to our fleet reflects in so many ways the striking interiors of those liners which were being designed in the opening days of the 20th century. Those of you who have been on board already, will know what I mean – the abundance of beautiful wood finishes, brass and marble; the tasteful use of stained glass; the luxurious soft furnishings; and her grand, double and triple-height public spaces, including her magnificent Royal Court Theatre complete with Royal Box. This is a pinnacle of ship design, equal only to the pinnacle of those first Cunard floating palaces.

"So, it is with great pleasure and pride, that I welcome all of you and especially Their Royal Highnesses, The Prince of Wales and The Duchess of Cornwall, to our very own dockside theatre, also with Royal Box, to celebrate our latest addition to the fleet in the continuing revival of a great shipping company – a shipping company with an unparalled history as will shortly unfold.

Thank you."

The distinguished actor Sir Derek Jacobi (right), playing the renowned explorer Phileas Fogg, then presented a short period piece setting the scene of the ambitious travellers of the Victorian era.

Mezzo Soprano Katherine Jenkins performed Gypsy Dance from Bizet's Carmen and the Choir of Winchester Cathedral sang Fauré's In Paradisum as the Naming Party made its way from the theatre's Royal Box to the stage.

The Lord Bishop of Winchester, The Right Reverend Michael Scott-Joynt, assisted by the Reverend Andrew Huckett, Port Chaplain, the Mission to Seafarers, offered the Prayers of Blessing.

After the prayers, the Master of Queen Victoria, Captain Paul Wright, invited The Duchess of Cornwall to perform the naming.

As the Duchess named the ship and said: "May God bless her and all who sail in her," she activated the release of a bottle of Veuve Clicquot champagne to smash against the side of the ship moored outside the transparent rear wall of the huge auditorium.

Cheers and applause from the invited audience and thousands of spectators watching a telecast in a nearby park, faltered slightly when the bottle failed to break after striking the side of the ship beneath its name.

Such occurrences stoke the fires of superstition and left one senior Carnival UK official to offer the following comment when later asked to foretell the future of the cruise industry over the next decade. "By 2020, we will hopefully have figured out a foolproof way of smashing champagne bottles on the side of our new ships."

Despite the setback and the obvious disappointment of the platform party, the spectacular event continued with a rendition of "I Saw Three Ships" by the three tenors Alfie Boe, Jon Christos and Gardar Thor Cortes accompanied by the Choir of Winchester Cathedral.

As Their Royal Highnesses departed, the Choir sand O Come All Ye Faithful in a rousing reminder that Queen Victoria was entering service two weeks before Christmas.

In Liverpool, on 26th July, HRH The Duchess of Cornwall is scheduled to make her first return to the ship she named.

Firework farewell for the new Cunarder

DECK BY DECK GUIDE

CUNARD LINE'S UNCOMPROMISING ATTENTION TO DETAIL
AND DESIGN LED TO BUILDING WORK ON THE FIRST QUEEN
VICTORIA BEING HALTED AND THE VESSEL UNDER
CONSTRUCTION IN ITALY ALLOCATED TO ANOTHER OF
CARNIVAL UK'S FAMOUS OPERATING BRANDS, P&O CRUISES.

The mighty Miami-based Carnival Corporation has a long association
with the Italian shipbuilders Fincantieri. Its yards have produced vessels
for a number of Carnival-owned lines including the subsidiary Carnival
Cruise Line; Costa; Holland America and Princess.

Carnival's shipbuilding teams have worked with their Italian
counterparts to develop various classes of cruise ship design. Orders for
new ships are often placed in batches for maximum cost effectiveness.

The order for the original Queen Victoria was announced on 31st March
2003 and a ceremony to mark the laying of her keel was held at the
Fincantieri yard the following July.

LEISURE AND RELAXATION

1 Connexion™ Conference Centre (Deck 3)

2 Cunard Royal Spa & Fitness Centre (Deck 9)

3 Cundaria Museum (Deck 2)

4 Empire Casino (Deck 2)

5 Images (Deck 3)

6 Library (Deck 2&3)

7 Hydropool – Cunard Royal Spa (Deck 9)

8 Lido pool (Deck 9)

9 Pavilion Pool (Deck 9)

10 Queens Arcade (Deck 2)

11 Sea Views Saunas – Cunard Royal Spa (Deck 9)

12 Sports Deck (Deck 11)

13 Royal Court Theatre (Decks 1, 2 & 3)

14 The Grand Lobby

15 The Grand Arcade – shops (Deck 3)

16 The Terrace (Deck 11)

17 The Zone and Play Zone (Deck 10)

18 Whirlpools – Lido Pool – aft (Deck 9)

19 Whirlpools – Pavilion Pool – aft (Deck 9)

20 The Grills upper Terrace (Deck12)

QUEEN VICTORIA

At that stage the detailed planning of how the public rooms on board the class of ship known as Vista started.

Cunard designers wanted to be sure the new vessel could provide guests with the Line's unique Grills experience – restaurants offering the finest dining at sea; sumptuous stateroom accommodation; private deck space and a lounge reserved for guests choosing to travel in the finest style.

Rather than compromise on the provision of these facilities on the Vista class ship on the drawing board, the decision was taken to halt work for Cunard Line and transfer the vessel under construction to P&O Cruises.

Overnight, the steel hull sitting in the dry dock at Fincantieri's Marghera yard near Venice became Arcadia, and new designs for Queen Victoria to be based on an enlarged Vista class design were started.

The liner design of Queen Victoria provided the ship's interior designers with more space in terms of height and volume.

Queen Victoria's Cunard heritage is reflected in the design of the grand, elegant and intimate public areas.

Guests embark into the ship's three-storey Grand Lobby decorated in mahogany and marble and featuring dramatic staircases with ornate wrought iron balustrade.

DINING VENUES

21 Britannia Restaurant (Deck 2 & 3)

THE GRILLS

22 Princess Grill Starboard side (Deck 11)

23 Queens Grill Port side (Deck 11)

24 The Courtyard (Deck 11)

25 The Grills Lounge (Deck 11)

OTHER DINING VENUES

26 Todd English Restaurant Port Side (Deck 2)

27 Winter Garden – Retractable Roof (Deck 9)

28 Lido (Deck 9)

BARS AND LOUNGES

29 Cafe Carinthia (Deck 2)

30 Chart Room (Deck 2)

31 Commodore Club (Deck 2)

32 Golden Lion (Deck 11)

33 Hemispheres (Deck 10)

34 Midships Bar and Lounge

35 The Queens Room (Deck 2 & 3)

36 Churchill's Cigar Lounge (Deck 10)

37 Admiral's Lounge (Deck 10)

A specially-commissioned art work spanning over 2½ decks in height symbolising the Cunard and Victoria historical style, and a dramatic ceiling with central feature chandelier are the striking focal points of Grand Lobby.

As on her sister Cunarders, each grade of stateroom is paired with a sea-view restaurant. The restaurants follow a similar pattern to QE2 and QM2. Grill Rooms are provided for the higher categories and a main restaurant for the deluxe and standard grades.

The main Dining Room, the Britannia Restaurant, spans two decks at the stern of the vessel, and evokes memories of classic ocean liner restaurants with sweeping staircases, art deco pillars and arches and a spectacular bronze and glass artwork centrepiece.

Both the Queens and Princess Grills are located on top of the ship, with exclusive access to Grill guests only.

It was Cunard Line's desire to give these restaurants their stunning location that led to the major change in design from the standard Vista class ship.

The result is impressive.

All Grill guests have the exclusive use of the Grills Lounge, conveniently located next to the Grills, and French doors open from each Grill onto The Courtyard – an exclusive patio area with steps to the Upper Grills Terrace – a secluded retreat on the ship's uppermost deck.

Decorated in creams and browns, the Queen's Grill is used by guests booked in the highest-grade staterooms and features the finest dining.

The intimate Princess Grill is for guests in Princess Suite staterooms.

Queen Victoria offers several alternative dining venues.

Todd English Restaurant, named after a renowned US chef; the informal Lido; Café Carinthia; the Golden Lion Pub and a Hamburger and Salad Bar.

*Royal Court Theatre
shown in all its glory*

Queen Victoria's three-deck Royal Court Theatre offers the first private boxes at sea, with a lounge area for guests to enjoy dessert and coffee before being escorted by uniformed bell boys to their box before the show.

The two-deck Queen's Room is the ship's ballroom designed for dancing, cocktail parties and traditional English afternoon teas complete with finger sandwiches – while fencing classes also take place here.

The spectacular room provides an ambience reminiscent of that enjoyed by Queen Victoria in her much loved Isle of Wight home Osborne House.

The room features crystal chandeliers, a large dance floor with inlaid wood patterns and backlit glass panels.

ConneXions Conference Centre and Internet Café comprise an education centre featuring a flexible classroom venue for programmes that include computer training, navigation, art and wine tasting.

Above, top: Winter Garden

Above: Britannia Restaurant

The Internet Café enables guests to stay in touch during their voyage as well as surf the web.

With its retractable glass roof, The Winter Garden is Queen Victoria's indoor / outdoor relaxation area and reminiscent of a grand conservatory complete with fountain.

Queen Victoria offers a range of bars and clubs (13 in total) to suit a wide variety of tastes and provide a range of atmospheres, including the Golden Lion pub, a Champagne Bar, a nautically-themed cocktail bar (The Chart Room) and the relaxing Midships Lounge.

A modern Casino features the latest machines, traditional tables and an accompanying bar.

The Royal Arcade shopping facility was inspired by both the Royal and Burlington Arcades in London.

Queen Victoria's Hemispheres room on top of the ship, overlooks the Pavilion Pool and is the venue for classes, lectures or just relaxation by day, before being transformed into a stunning nightclub in the evening.

The Commodore Club observation lounge features a full bar and sweeping views over the bow of Queen Victoria.

Adjacent to this room is the Admiral's Lounge and Churchill's Cigar Lounge.

The 6,000 book traditionally-styled English Library, situated over two decks, features rich mahogany wood panelling, stained glass, leather sofas and armchairs and a spiral staircase. A bookshop complements the library.

Queen Victoria also features a floating museum called Cunardia displaying a unique collection of Cunard memorabilia and artefacts.

Child facilities on board are among the finest afloat.

The Cunard Royal Spa and Fitness centre features the latest spa and beauty treatments for both men and women, as well as a hydro-pool and thermal suite.

Next to the Spa and Treatment Rooms, there's an expansive gymnasium and aerobics area with state-of-the-art cardiovascular fitness equipment including inclining treadmills and bikes complete with their own personal LCD television screens.

Other than the large hydro-pool in the Spa, there are two outdoor swimming pools.

In a little more than two-and-half years in service, Queen Victoria's crew have helped establish the ship as a favourite among Cunard Line guests, many of whom have transferred their affection from Queen Elizabeth 2 following her sale to developers in Dubai.

Top: The Casino

Middle: Hydro-pool and Spa

Bottom: English Library, which spans two decks

WELCOME RETURN OF THE WORLD'S GREATEST LINERS

QE2 TAKES HONOURS IN HER SPIRITUAL HOME

THE MOST FAMOUS AND SUCCESSFUL CUNARD LINER IN HISTORY MARKED THE OFFICIAL OPENING OF LIVERPOOL'S PIER HEAD CRUISE BERTH IN 2007.

Queen Elizabeth 2 took centre stage at the £19m landing stage adjacent to Princes Dock – navigating the same stretches of the Mersey that were so familiar to so many of her sister ships in previous decades.

The call was QE2's eighth to the city where Cunard Line started its transatlantic service in 1840, and marked the great ocean liner's penultimate visit to the Line's spiritual home. Since that celebration, during which HRH The Duke of Kent (right) marked the official opening of the berth, more than 30 cruise ships have come alongside at Liverpool's world famous waterfront, part of the city's UNESCO World Heritage Site waterfront.

View of the old Terminal from the Cunard Building

The multi-million pound regeneration of the city centre and its waterfront, together with its unique mercantile, sporting and musical heritage, have ensured fond memories live long in the minds of visitors arriving on board some of he world's largest cruise ships.

And the feedback they provide has been overwhelmingly positive with many citing the call at Liverpool as a leading reason they book their cruise.

The successful re-emergence of Liverpool as a port of call for the liners has also generated a significant economic benefit for the city and wider region. It is estimated that passengers arriving aboard the 17 ships calling at Pier Head during 2010 will pour at least £1.9m into the local economy.

This positive economic impact increases when spectator spend is calculated. But despite its appeal to visitors and popularity with many of the world's leading ship operators, the city has still to resolve the regulatory difficulties preventing the berth being used as a full turnaround facility for itineraries starting and ending at Liverpool.

The Crown Princess, berthed at the Cruise Liner terminal

Liverpool City Council's Director of Regeneration John Kelly says:

"Over the past few years, there has been a concerted effort to bring life back to the Mersey waterfront. Taking the opportunity to use European and other public funding sources some £300m has been invested in major schemes such as the Arena and Convention Centre, the Pier Head public realm works and canal link and the Museum of Liverpool.

"Private investment is heavily in evidence now too. Downing Development have carried out a £10m refurbishment of the Port of Liverpool building, new hotels have been opened and Peel Developments have major planning applications in train for £6bn of investment over the next 30 years.

"A catalyst for much of this development however, was the cruise liner terminal. It showed our determination to bring major vessels back to the Mersey on a regular basis.

"While we estimate that our economy has been directly boosted by £13m from these visitors, the public relations value of so many visitors, spreading the word about Liverpool's renaissance, is incalculable.

"The best thing of all about the Cruise Liner Terminal is that, more than anything else, it has come to symbolise the self-confidence and pride of the city."

THE FULL 2010 SCHEDULE OF CRUISE SHIP CALLS:

Date	Vessel	Pax	Cruise line
23.5.10	AAURA	1266	Aida
2/3.6.10	DEUTSCHLAND	548	Peter Dielman
6.6.10	AAURA	1266	Aida
19.6.10	CRYSTAL SYMPHONY	960	Crystal
26.6.10	THE DISCOVERY	796	
27.6.10	CROWN PRINCESS	3114	Princess
10.7.10	AAURA	1266	Aida
21.7.10	CROWN PRINCESS	3114	Princess
24.7.10	AAURA	1266	Aida
26.7.10	QUEEN VICTORIA	2014	Cunard
5.8.10	ASTOR	590	Transocean
8.8.10	MAASDAM	1200	Holland America
14.8.10	CROWN PRINCESS	3114	Princess
16-19.8.10	THE WORLD	200	Residensea
22.8.10	AZAMARA	694	Azamara/Celebrity
26.8.10	CROWN PRINCESS	3114	Princess
30.8.10	WESTERDAM	1900	Holland America

Queen Mary 2 turns in the Mersey on her maiden visit to Liverpool. Picture by Andrew Teebay

CUNARD'S UNIQUE BOND WITH THE RIVER MERSEY

LIVERPOOL IS THE SPIRITUAL HOME OF CUNARD AND, WHEREVER IN THE WORLD THE COMPANY HAPPENS TO BE BASED, WILL ALWAYS BE SO.

Peter Shanks, Cunard Line President and Managing Director (left), shares the passion of his predecessors for the city's rich maritime heritage and its unique position in the 170-year history of the line he now runs.

"We have something very special in the relationship between Liverpool and Cunard Line," he says.

The most famous and successful Cunarder in history – the legendary QE2 – was planned and designed in the Cunard Building at the Pier Head.

By the time she entered service in 1969, the Head office had moved to New York and the operations base was at Southampton.

Liverpool had to wait 21 years before being able to welcome the transatlantic queen to the city of its conception.

It was worth the wait. More than 1 million people turned out on the banks of the Mersey throughout the day and evening of Tuesday, 24th July 1990 during QE2's maiden call at Liverpool.

The magnificent liner visited the Mersey a further eight times before being retired from Cunard Line service in November 2008.

Each of her visits generated high levels of excitement and interest.

Between that maiden call and 2007, the 963ft-long liner with a gross tonnage of 70,327 dropped anchor mid-Mersey, her 32ft 7.5in draught accommodated in the high and fast flowing range of the river.

Throughout these visits Mersey Ferries provided a tender service for guests and crew to reach the shore at Pier Head. One visit coincided with Liverpool's annual homage to its most famous four sons – the Mathew Street Festival and International Beatle Week convention.

Unsuspecting guests disembarking their Mersey Ferry at Pier Head were immediately cast into a throng of thousands of music fans enjoying the free open air concerts on specially erected stages throughout the city centre.

Stilt walkers in Sgt Pepper costumes welcomed QE2 passengers ashore while from the bridge the music-hating Blue Meanie, made famous in the band's Yellow Submarine film, stood surveying the scene ashore.

If QE2 arrivals at Liverpool were impressive, her departures became the stuff of legend – punctuated by some of the most spectacular waterfront firework displays the city has ever staged.

On one occasion, in July 2000, QE2's scheduled departure from the Mersey coincided with the start of a sell-out concert by Sir Elton John who took to the stage in the waterfront's temporary "Big Top" tented arena as the ship's whistle sounded.

The star, a past guest on board, acknowledged the presence of the luxurious liner as he started his concert.

Seven years later, during her visit in September 2007, QE2 attracted even more attention and took centre stage at the opening of the long-awaited City of Liverpool cruise ship berth at Princes Parade.

For the first time, on September 21st that year, QE2 was able to berth alongside at Liverpool, almost within the shadows of Cunard Line's former headquarters at Pier Head.

The thousands of spectators that day were able to truly gauge the size and spectacle of the liner as she sat alongside one of the world's most famous waterfronts.

With a close-up view available for the first time in Liverpool, the most successful ocean liner in history won thousands of new fans among the flag-waving well-wishers who lined the waterfront all day and well into the night.

A little over a year later it was time for Liverpool to say goodbye to its favourite adopted ship.

QE2 arrived in the Mersey off the Pier Head a little after 11am on Friday, 3rd October 2008, marking the start of a day of celebration and sad farewells.

In line with maritime custom QE2 flew her magnificent 39 foot-long paying-off pennant from her mast as her Master Captain Ian McNaught, assisted by a Liverpool Pilot, edged the liner towards her Liverpool berth for the last time.

The pennant is the longest in Cunard Line history – one foot for each year the famous liner was in service. Later that day it was presented to the city of Liverpool during a special farewell concert at the Anglican Cathedral.

QE2's final farewell that evening was watched by tens of thousands of spectators on both sides of the River Mersey – out to witness the end of another chapter in the enduring 170-year history linking Liverpool and Cunard Line.

Crowds gather to record the event.

The next chapter opened a little more than a year later.

On Tuesday, 20th October 2009, Liverpool prepared to welcome the largest ocean liner in the world. Cunard Line's flagship Queen Mary 2 was to make her inaugural call at the city as part of a fifth birthday lap of honour circumnavigation of the British Isles.

She let go of her ropes at Southampton's Ocean terminal shortly after 5pm the previous Thursday bound for South Queensferry in the Firth of Forth near Edinburgh.

Tugs at the Liner's homeport joined the celebrations by providing a fire hose salute as the mighty Cunarder reversed away from her berth. It was a first leg voyage of 460 nautical miles. Throughout Friday Commodore Bernard Warner and his Bridge team navigated a course close to famous east coast landmarks and resorts along the shore of Yorkshire and Northumberland. Off Spurn Head, at the mouth of the River Humber, QM2 took a course towards the famous Flamborough Head and, beyond, Scarborough.

Strong winds and a heavy sea prevented many small private and pleasure craft from joining the sail past, but ashore thousands of well-wishers were visible from QM2's vast open decks. Car headlights flashed and horns were sounded as the liner made her majestic way north.

QM2's 5th anniversary lap of honour round the UK

*Crowds spent the day
at Princes Parade*

Long blasts on the ship's whistle punctuated the passage along the famous stretch of coastline. At Whitby crowds could be seen in the grounds of the resort's famous cliff-top ruins while at nearby Sandsend more crowds had waited patiently on the beach to view the ship.

The vessel passed the distinctive twin quays at the mouth of the River Tyne shortly before sunset on Friday evening, and helicopters and light aircraft followed her course north.

The Farne Islands, off Bamburgh in Northumberland came and went as QM2 continued her progress towards the Forth.

At sunrise on the Saturday QM2 was nearing her anchorage in the shadow of the famous Forth Railway Bridge at South Queensferry.

Throughout the day, thousands of spectators descended on the waterfront to catch sight of the liner during only her second call at the Edinburgh landmark.

Shortly after 6pm the order was given for the ship to set off for Greenock, a distance of 594 nautical miles.

The following day was spent in spectacular coastal scenery. Early in the morning, QM2 rounded Rottery Head on a north-westerly heading towards Duncansby Head, entering Pentland Firth and passing between the Island of Stroma and South Ronaldsay.

Shortly after breakfast the island of Hoy, dominated by the famous Old Man of Hoy, came into view.

The ship then headed towards Cape Wrath before entering the North Minch, passing between the Isle of Lewis and the west coast of Scotland.

A short time later, in brilliant sunshine QM2 entered the Little Minch between the Isle of Harris and Isle of Skye, and onwards towards the Hebrides.

The following morning, Queen Mary 2 arrived on the Clyde – scene over the years of more than 120 Cunard liner launches. Before sunrise at Greenock thousands of well-wishers had gathered to welcome the ship on her maiden call. As day broke they were joined by dozens of small craft on the waters around the ships' berth at Clydeport.

That evening, QM2 departed the Clyde, former home to the famous shipyards of John Brown.

Glasgow's place in Cunard history is firmly established and survives despite the fact the last liner in the fleet to be built there was QE2, launched off John Brown's slipway by Her Majesty the Queen in September 1967.

Once again, tens of thousands of spectators lined the promenade of the proud industrial town as the mighty, 148,000 ton flagship set off bound for Liverpool. Pipers on the dockside were drowned out by another firework spectacular, greeted with loud cheers from QM2's packed open decks and the crowded vantage points ashore.

On board that evening the sense of excitement about the following day's arrival in Liverpool grew. By the time most guests surfaced from their staterooms for breakfast (or had enjoyed their first meal of the day as room service) QM2 was making good speed off the Anglesey coast.

The weather was fair with a stiff breeze across the open decks.

On the bridge Commodore Bernard Warner – making his first call by ship to the port of Liverpool – and his team prepared for the spectacular arrival at Pier Head.

Commodore Bernard Warner aboard Queen Mary 2

Plans had been drawn up for the longest, widest, tallest (and grandest!) ocean liner in the world to turn in mid-Mersey to berth "starboard on" at Liverpool.

Painstaking calculations of tidal range and depth of water had also been made – in the first instance to make sure the huge ship could pass the Mersey bar safely and then to ensure she could be safely tied up at the berth. Intensive dredging of the river bed around the berth had been carried out in the days before the visit.

Before the ship reached that final resting point for the day she had to pass through a flotilla of welcoming craft. Tugs, lifeboats, speed boats, private launches, jet skis and a packed Mersey Ferry Royal Daffodil passed as close as they dare to the mighty liner as she made her way between Crosby beach and Fort Perch Rock at New Brighton.

The Wirral promenade was thronged with spectators and light aircraft and film helicopters bussed overhead.

Tugs in attendance switched on their fire hoses in salute – at one stage drenching unsuspecting passengers on the liner's open decks.

With one of the highest and fastest flowing tidal ranges in Britain, the Mersey commands both concentration and respect from those navigating its waters.

Commodore Warner and his team had worked with Liverpool Pilot Chris Booker to plan the arrival – and the intricate mid-river turn.

On board the first signs that the turn was underway became apparent sooner than many guests had expected.

Shortly after passing Wallasey Town Hall and the Wirral promenade at Egremont, those paying attention on board became aware of what those ashore could see for themselves: the giant liner was turning.

The manoeuvre was a complex piece of expert seamanship delivered to perfection. With the tide running at four knots, QM2 was allowed to drift gently to the landing stage.

By 1145 she was alongside and secure a short while later marking the start of another remarkable day for Cunard and the City of Liverpool.

Peter Shanks later offered his own reflections on the historic day.

"It was hard to imagine after the spectacular departure from Greenock the night before that things could get any better – but they did.

Queen Mary 2
during a 180 degree turn
along the River Mersey

"My start to the day was on the bridge as we sailed into the River Mersey. There was a strong tide with us pushing the ship along. As we neared the centre of the city it became clear why the day was going to be so special – many thousands of people had come out to greet us.

"In front of us were the famous Three Graces buildings and from the central building, the Cunard building, flew the Cunard house flag.

"I don't think the people of Liverpool knew what to think as the mammoth Queen Mary 2 performed a perfect 180 degree turn as she came down on the tide – ending up perfectly in line with the berth. I am not sure how many times the ship's whistle blew – but there was no doubting we had arrived.

"I stepped off the ship with Commodore Warner to a frenzy of local TV and radio interviews. Perhaps the most fun interview was with Sky Sports. They were in town for the big Liverpool v Lyon football match that evening. They had come down to film Queen Mary 2 and ask the Commodore who he thought would win. He predicted a 3-1 win for Liverpool – then went on to say he was a Leeds supporter.

"The day then unfolded with a series of events including a Plaque Exchange – we invited the Lord Mayor of Liverpool Cllr Mike Storey on board with local dignitaries for lunch. We also invited the local Royal National Lifeboat Institute (RNLI) on for a tour of the ship and afternoon tea. We are big supporters of all they do and it is right we are able to repay them in a small way for all that they do.

"After the Commodore and I had said a few words of welcome, they said they had something for us. Up stepped a beautiful young girl. She gingerly walked up to the two of us, looked up and said 'I was born on 8 January 2004 – I have the same birthday as Queen Mary 2' – and then handed Commodore a birthday card for the ship. Well, we were speechless, what a lovely and unexpected moment!

*Mersey Ferry
Royal Daffodil
passes QM2*

"Of course we recovered our composure and sent for some Cunard teddy bears to give in return. That has to be the best Plaque Exchange I have witnessed.

"I suspected all along that what we had planned for the evening would work but could never have expected such a fine concert. The Royal Court Theatre on board was packed for two shows in the evening. We had 63 members of the Royal Liverpool Philharmonic on stage, the wonderful soprano Helen Williams, the famous tenor Jon Christos and of course our good friend and conductor Anthony Inglis.

"Anthony took the audience through the concert with a script depicting the history of Cunard Line, Liverpool and of course Queen Mary 2. The music included just what you would expect: The National Anthem – yes we sang all the verses; Song of the Clyde – Jon sang this famous tune depicting ships and the Clyde; Orpheus in the Underworld – by Offenbach, the orchestra were stunning; You'll Never Walk Alone – Oh my goodness (on Queen Mary 2, on the Mersey – awesome!); Queen of the Sea – a wonderful song all about the original Queen Mary; Battle Hymn of the Republic – this had our American guests enthralled; Happy Birthday – we all sang happy birthday Queen Mary 2 and Jerusalem – works every time and the singing by the audience was terrific!

"And if that wasn't enough – out came the expected Union Jack flags as we finished with Pomp and Circumstance and Land of Hope and Glory.

"We have had some big nights in the Royal Court Theatre over the last 5 years – Shirley Bassey, James Taylor, Skellern and Stilgoe, Lesley Garrett – well this was right up there with the best of them and left everybody feeling inspired.

"We had the best Beatles tribute band in the country on board and later that evening they played two concerts to a packed Queens Room.

"The ship sailed at 2300 hours. We were amazed at the tens of thousands of people lining the river. They had come down to wave goodbye to Queen Mary 2. A wonderful firework display lit up the night, Queen Mary 2 slipped off the berth and we sailed out of Liverpool down the Mersey. It was not 'Goodbye'.

"Queen Mary 2 will return to Cunard Line's spiritual home many, many more times in the future."

"THANK YOU LIVERPOOL – YOU DID US PROUD!"
CUNARD LINE PRESIDENT
PETER SHANKS

SERVIA
~1881~

Robert Lloyd, Marine Artist

MASTER OF
THE CUNARD ART

ROBERT LLOYD IS A MARINE ARTIST WITH A WORLDWIDE
REPUTATION FOR PRODUCING VISUALLY STUNNING AND
TECHNICALLY ACCURATE PAINTINGS FOR THE MARINE
INDUSTRY, PRIVATE INDIVIDUALS AND MUSEUM COLLECTIONS.

His critically-acclaimed portfolio includes a number of stunning
commissions completed for Cunard Line.

His interest in the sea started during his childhood in Wirral.

"During school summer holidays I used to go with my mother to New
Brighton promenade to watch the ships going in and out of Liverpool. This
was in the late 1970s and early 80s and there really wasn't much to see
apart from the occasional coaster or Isle of Man Steam Packet ferry. If I
was lucky, I would see an ACL container ship coming in or leaving," he
recalls.

"I was fascinated even at that age, where had they come from? Where were they going? What were they carrying? The questions used to go through my mind all the time.

"Like all children, I used to like drawing – I remember drawing a lot of lorries and tanks and battles. This was something friends did too at school. It wasn't until later in secondary school when any real indication of ability became obvious," explains Robert.

"I had been on a trip up the Manchester Ship Canal on one of the Mersey Ferries, and had taken some photos at the oil terminal at Eastham of a tanker.

"Then my art teacher, Mr Hill, had set a project to do a painting for a competition at school so I decided to paint that tanker.

"Whilst I was painting it, I had shown her at sea rather than in dock. My teacher came up to me and made a comment that has stuck with me ever since. He said, 'the sea is never completely blue, there are always lots of colours, greens, blues and browns' in the case of the River Mersey then. Perhaps that was the turning point. I started to add in different colours and finished the painting. It won the competition, ten pounds I think I won, and it was exhibited at the Library at the Concourse in West Kirby."

Growing up on a peninsular influenced the young artist.

"Being surrounded by sea on three sides on Wirral obviously had a major influence on my interest in shipping and the sea. From my bedroom window I could see the Bar Light ship which I suppose was about 15 miles away. I could see the ships passing and anchored and those same thoughts used to come to mind. I could also see Hilbre Island and the Dee Estuary and would often see small coasters and occasionally a Trinity House Tender negotiating the twisting channels out of the Estuary.

Top: HM The Queen inspects the artist's final painting of QE2

Below: Cunard's Three Queens in Southampton Water

"I was a member of the Sea Scouts and would often sail into the Estuary and sail up to the navigation Buoys. I spent many afternoons and evenings sailing and canoeing on the Marine Lake in West Kirby and the estuary and loved the feeling of being on the water."

For the inquisitive teenager fascinated by ships, Birkenhead Docks proved a major attraction.

"I often went down to Birkenhead Docks to have a look around. Security in those days was virtually non-existent and I used to wander around looking at these huge ships, often laid up. Everything seemed to be on such a huge scale."

The Mersey Ferries also proved a popular draw for the youngster.

"I would often sail back and forth on the Mersey Ferries; windy rough days were the best, rolling all over the place. I always enjoyed rough weather, and still do. I recall a particularly rough crossing to the Isle of Man on a family holiday. It was on one of the old steamers. It was probably only a force 6 or 7 but the ferry was rolling and pitching all over the place. Most of the passengers seemed to have disappeared, there was hardly anyone on deck, but I loved it. The wind was moaning in the rigging and the spray

A final commission to paint QE2 is placed on board the fomer flagship

was coming right across the decks. It was for me a wonderful experience although it did teach me to carefully observe the other passengers; I was careful to always stay well up wind of anyone who looked even slightly green!"

As the time to leave school approached Robert was considering a career at sea.

"I had decided to pursue a career at sea. However, my careers teacher suggested that perhaps I would have a better future if I pursued a career in art and went to Art College instead. A friend of mine was already at Art College, Withens Lane in Wallasey, so that's what I ended up doing. I was at Withens Lane for three years studying graphics and illustration and then went on to study industrial and three dimensional design at a college outside London. At this point all thoughts of the sea had pretty much disappeared and after leaving college I joined an advertising agency working for the likes of Virgin, Proctor & Gamble, Phillip Morris and Chrysalis producing brochures, record covers and so on."

Among the clients of the advertising agency was P&O Ferries.

"Knowing my interest in fine art painting, they asked me to produce a painting of one of their new ferries, the Pride of Portsmouth. Then they commissioned two more and made a number of introductions to other shipping companies who all seemed interested in having me produce paintings for them. I eventually gave up working in advertising and started to paint full time."

Over the years he has painted a wide range of shipping subjects for companies, museums and individuals all over the world. The subjects have ranged from oil tankers to oil rigs, cruise ships and liners to ferries and container ships.

"Probably my most challenging commission to date has been a series of paintings rather than one individual painting," he reveals.

"Over the last two years I have working on a series of 40 paintings for a company called Qatargas. They had under construction what was the largest ever peace-time order for ships. To give a comparison, Cunard's Queen Victoria weighs 90,000 tons, not small by any measure, but these gas carriers weigh in at 220,000 tons and are over 300 metres in length.

"They are Liquid Natural Gas carriers and although they had some technical differences, they were essentially very similar in appearance. The challenge was not only the number of paintings to complete but to ensure that each painting showed a different view and background. That's easy enough for five paintings but a great deal of thought and research has to be put in for 40!"

The multiple commissions proved a satisfying assignment, but it is a painting of the former Cunard Line flagship Queen Elizabeth 2 that gave the artist most satisfaction.

He explains: "The painting was entitled 'Coming Home' and showed her sailing up Southampton Water on her final call before sailing off to Dubai. She is shown at a very impressive angle looking sleek and handsome. It was quite a large painting, about 7ft wide by 4ft deep. It was commissioned by Cunard to celebrate this most historic of Liners and was unveiled by Her Majesty the Queen on board in Southampton."

The painting was displayed on board the QE2 until she made the final call to Southampton – the arrival depicted in the painting. On his final farewell visit to the ship HRH The Duke of Edinburgh presented the work to the City of Southampton.

Robert's association with Cunard Line started after a meeting with Liverpool-born retired Commodore Ron Warwick.

"I was first introduced to Cunard by Commodore Ron Warwick, having just completed a painting for him of the QE2. He was master at the time and he invited me onboard whilst the ship was in Southampton."

Since then he has completed around a dozen paintings for Cunard.

"The first one completed was presented to Margaret Thatcher to commemorate the QE2's part in the Falklands War. I believe she has this painting hung in her drawing room at home. I've also completed paintings of the Queen Mary 2 as well as a number of other paintings for various occasions."

He is currently working on a number of paintings for the new Cunard Liner Queen Elizabeth.

"There are conventional paintings which feature historic Cunard Ships such as the original Queen Elizabeth as well as two very large paintings – 16ft x 5ft. One depicts the QE2, QM2 and the Queen Victoria when they met in Southampton in 2008, and the other shows the Queen Elizabeth entering Sydney Harbour."

During special celebration voyages around the British Isles completed by both QE2 and QM2, Robert has sailed on board, painting and completing a work featuring the ship.

"I very much enjoy completing the paintings on board the ships. I don't deny that it can get a little stressful as there can sometimes be quite a large crowd and you can have a lot of questions all at the same time. It would also be true to say that I don't make much progress whilst working in public.

Queen Victoria leaving Venice

"I don't mind the questions, it is after all why I am there, although some questions can get a bit repetitive like 'how long will it take to finish?' or 'where do you start?' and 'do you paint by numbers!?'".

He adds: "You do meet some very interesting people from all walks of life many of whom have served at sea or like me are simply fascinated by ships and the sea. The only time when painting in public on board the ships can get a little difficult is when there are rough seas. You tend to sway with the motion of the ships which makes it a little difficult to paint a straight line, but actually helps when you are painting the sea. I did once have a passenger stumble directly into the painting when we hit a large wave, fortunately there was no damage either to the painting or the passenger although he did look a little surprised – he had obviously not noticed me, the crowd or the painting."

Robert's works hanging on board Queen Victoria are among the most striking on the ship.

"The most prominent are two murals depicting Cunard's first steam-powered ship Britannia and another featuring the Servia," he says.

"I will always be indebted to Eric Flounders and Michael Gallagher at Cunard for entrusting me with the various paintings I have completed for them, as well as Commodore Warwick for making that first introduction all those years ago in the Captain's Cabin on board the QE2."

COMING SOON...

ART DECO FLOURISHES, RICH WOOD PANELLING, INTRICATE MOSAICS, GLEAMING CHANDELIERS AND COOL MARBLES WILL COMBINE TO GIVE QUEEN ELIZABETH A UNIQUE DESIGN AND PERSONALITY OF HER OWN – BUT A STYLE THAT FITS PERFECTLY WITH THAT FOUND ON HER SISTER OCEAN LINERS QUEEN MARY 2 AND QUEEN VICTORIA.

Queen Elizabeth is likely to impress as soon as guests embark into the ship's triple height Grand Lobby, which will showcase the grandeur of the ship and link her with ocean liners of the past.

With its finishes of light mahogany and marble, stunning art deco chandeliers from the era of the first Queen Elizabeth, cantilevered balconies and a magnificent two-deck-high original artwork piece on the grand staircase, the Grand Lobby is the social focal point of the ship.

Cunard ships, while among the most modern afloat, are known for their traditional luxury, accentuated by extensive use of brass, classic fabrics, marble and highly polished woods and veneers.

no-one was better qualified for this detailed but monumental work than the company of the exceptional craftsman David Linley, whose creative ability and mastery of wood is renowned".

As a result, Linley, a company specialising in the design and manufacture of fine furniture and marquetry was commissioned to design and make this stunning centrepiece at the heart of the ship. Work is currently under way, and the completed panel will be shipped during the summer to the Fincantieri shipyard at Monfalcone, Italy, where it will be installed over a period of four days to take pride of place just before the ship enters service in October.

The magnificent artwork shows the port bow of the original Queen Elizabeth seen dramatically from sea level, and is intricately executed using the technique of marquetry inlay in nine different types of wood veneers. Spanning 2½ decks, the panel is made up of nine panels seamlessly jointed to lightweight board.

The marquetry panel features Madrona, Indian ebony, American walnut, grey ripple sycamore, burr ash, bird's eye maple, satin walnut, ash, burr walnut and Macassar ebony – all used to depict the evocative image of Queen Elizabeth.

Commenting on the challenges faced by the bespoke commission, Linley's Chairman, David Linley, who founded the company in 1985, said: "Though we have made fittings for luxury yachts in the past, this is the first sea-going work we have done on this scale – it is certainly the largest screen we have ever made – but it was a commission I was delighted to accept. I recall my father saying the interior design on Cunard's Queen Elizabeth 2 made one proud to be British, so I am hoping our achievement on the new Queen Elizabeth will make him – and others – equally proud".

Above: The Linley panel as it will hang in Queen Elizabeth's Grand Lobby

Cunard's President and Managing Director, Peter Shanks, says: "We needed to fill that space with a decorative screen which would not just be dramatic, a 'wow' factor in an area already full of 'wow', but which would also reflect our emphasis on traditional and sumptuous materials. After much thought and exploratory work, it was decided to commission a 5.6-metre (18ft 6in) high marquetry panel depicting the original Queen Elizabeth, an Art Deco icon, using a variety of natural woods from around the world.

"Once we had decided on the theme and the medium, it didn't take us long to conclude that

Queen Elizabeth will be the second largest Cunarder ever built and will join her sisters Queen Mary 2 and Queen Victoria as part of the youngest fleet in the world.

From the outside, her distinctive black and red livery will hint at an experience that differentiates a Cunard liner from a modern-day cruise ship. This will be most evident in the ship's adherence to liner traditions, with elegant double and triple height public rooms on a grand scale, luxuriously endowed with rich wood panelling, intricate mosaics, hand-woven carpets, gleaming chandeliers and cool marbles. Art Deco features will pay homage to the original Queen Elizabeth, and will allow the new ship to reflect a more civilized era of travel.

Plaques detailing the Captains who have served on the two previous Cunard Elizabeths will celebrate the continuation of the 'Elizabeth' name, and a third plaque will record over time the names of the future masters of the new Queen Elizabeth.

DINING

As on her sisters, each grade of stateroom is paired with a sea-view restaurant. The restaurants will follow a similar pattern to Cunard's other ships, with Grill Rooms for the higher suites and a main restaurant for the deluxe grades – this ship will have a Britannia Club for the top grade balcony guests. Cuisine will be to the excellent Cunard standards, delivered with our exclusive White Star Service in all dining areas.

The main Dining Room, the Britannia Restaurant, is destined to be one of the most remarkable rooms at sea, spanning two decks at the stern of the vessel and offering a true Art Deco feel. It will evoke memories of classic ocean liner restaurants with a unique sweeping staircase and marbleised backlit decorative ceiling among the focal points. Breakfast and lunch will be served in an open sitting and guests have the option of either main or late sitting for dinner.

Both the Queen's and Princess Grills will be located on top of the ship (Deck 11), enclosed by graceful and gently curving panoramic glass walls on the seaboard sides, and cantilevered out over the side of the vessel above Deck 10. There will be exclusive access to Grill guests only. Both Grills will offer a single sitting, so guests can enter at a time of their choosing, and the restaurants themselves, although architecturally similar, will be differently decorated to create an individual feel.

Grills guests will also have exclusive use of their own private lounge and bar conveniently located next to the Grills restaurants, and complete with resident Concierge.

French–style doors will open from each Grill onto the Courtyard – an exclusive patio area – where al fresco dining will be offered, and steps will lead up to the Grills Terrace, a secluded

Above: The Queen's Grill

Above: Royal Court Theatre

Above, middle: Cafe Carinthia

Top: The Garden Lounge conservatory

retreat that's on the ship's uppermost deck where Grills guests can enjoy luxurious sun beds and exclusive waiter service.

In addition Queen Elizabeth will offer several alternative dining venues:

The Garden Lounge, also named after a room on the first Queen Elizabeth, will host occasional evening 'Supper Clubs' with musical entertainment and dancing. The area will have a palm–filled conservatory feel inspired by the glass houses at Kew Gardens and its vaulted glass ceiling will make it a truly light, bright and airy place to sit by day.

The alternative restaurant on Deck 2. Further details will be released on this in due course. This will be an open seating restaurant, where guests will make reservations for a time and day of their choosing, and a nominal additional charge will apply.

The Lido Restaurants, up on Deck 9 will be light spacious areas with wonderful sea views, and will offer breakfast and lunch buffet style. In the evenings two of the restaurants will serve different styles of regional cuisine, in a more formal setting, and the third will continue to offer an extensive buffet.

The extensive Cafe Carinthia will continue the popular concept introduced on Queen Victoria and offer Art Deco touches and rich décor whilst guests enjoy sweet pastries and fine teas and coffees. The Golden Lion Pub, another Cunard tradition, will offer traditional English pub food for lunch in a typical British pub setting.

ENTERTAINMENT

The magnificent three-deck Royal Court Theatre, with tiered seating for 832 guests, will be the location for the main entertainment of the evening with full-scale, West End-style productions as well as named entertainers. Decorated in a regal blue and gold colour scheme, this grand auditorium will offer private boxes on the upper level along with a lounge area for guests to enjoy drinks before the show. They can then enjoy champagne and petit fours or chocolates in their box during the show, ringing for service as they wish on their private (and silent!) velvet bell pull.

Queen Elizabeth's two-deck Queen's Room ballroom, another Cunard signature feature, is designed for dancing, cocktail parties and traditional English afternoon teas complete with finger sandwiches and freshly baked scones with jam and cream.